D0090616

UNLOCKING GREATNESS

THE UNEXPECTED JOURNEY
FROM THE LIFE YOU HAVE
TO THE LIFE YOU WANT

UNLOCKING
GREATNESS

CHARLIE HARARY

with Mark Dagostino

RODALE

RODALE *wellness*

Live happy. Be healthy. Get inspired.

Sign up today to get exclusive access to our authors, exclusive bonuses, and the most authoritative, useful, and cutting-edge information on health, wellness, fitness, and living your life to the fullest.

Visit us online at RodaleWellness.com
Join us at RodaleWellness.com/Join

Rodale books may be purchased for business or promotional use or for special sales. For information, please e-mail: BookMarketing@Rodale.com.
Printed in the United States of America
Rodale Inc. makes every effort to use acid-free ♾, recycled paper ♻.

Book design by Amy King

Library of Congress Cataloging-in-Publication Data is on file with the publisher.

ISBN 978-1-62336-976-7

Distributed to the trade by Macmillan

2 4 6 8 10 9 7 5 3 1 hardcover

We inspire health, healing, happiness, and love in the world.
Starting with you.

To my loving wife
caring parents
precious children
and
empowering God.
Thank you for being in my life.
I am who I am because of you.

CONTENTS

INTRODUCTION

Why Am I Perpetually Unsatisfied?

W hat do you want?"

The silent pause after I posed that question seemed to blot out every other noise in the city.

We had been sitting at Starbucks for over an hour. I was on my second Venti-size refill. Outside, a sea of pedestrians weaved hurriedly around the nearly stationary pillars of tourists who clogged the sidewalks gawking at tall buildings and dazzled by lights. It struck me that even Starbucks is different in New York City. It adapts to keep up with the intensity. Customers move as if on an assembly line, shouting complex orders of made-up coffee names while maintaining conversations on their earpieces and simultaneously checking their smartphones.

Dave and I sat by the window. He'd asked me to meet him here to talk about problems he was having at work. He wanted my advice, he said. But our conversation quickly turned to a discussion about the unhappy state of his family and then to himself.

Dave was my college buddy. Back in the day, if I were a betting man I would have bet the house that Dave would be running the world by the time he was 40. He wasn't just smart; he was *mad* smart. He also happened to be good-looking, athletic, and comfortable being the center of attention. Yet now, as he approached his 40th birthday, his life was unraveling. His job as a Wall Street banker had stalled, his marriage was on the rocks, and his three kids—well, let's just say he might still have a chance with his youngest.

He had achieved what so many people consider "the dream," complete with a picture-perfect family, a beautiful home, a distinguished career, and season tickets to his favorite team. Yet now, to him, it felt like it was all falling apart. Dave came to me trying to help plug a hole in what seemed like the breaking of a dam.

What he didn't realize was that he already had the power to not only to plug the hole, but stop the crumbling altogether; to build a much stronger, more powerful dam, complete with a turbine to reenergize everything he wanted out of life.

The question he needed to answer first, though, was: "What do you want?"

"I told you," he said. "To make more money, to improve my marriage, to—"

"No," I cut him off. I didn't want to hear some recitation of *everyone's* life goals. "Can you dig a little deeper?" I pushed. "Stop saying the things you are supposed to say. You have so much and yet so little. You have what looks like a really great life, and you're miserable. *Why?* What is it you really want but don't have?"

Silence.

With all of my training as an attorney, I have a hard time letting silence linger, especially when I sense weakness. But I let it sit there as the lightning-paced world around us seemed to fade away.

"I don't know," he finally said.

"That's your problem," I responded, smiling as if I had just helped him.

We wouldn't come to an answer that day. The noise of the crowd rushed back in, and the conversation ended with Dave feeling rather deflated. I promised we would follow up. I told him he had made a great start. Admitting that he didn't know what he wanted and that he didn't really know how to fix any of his problems was the start of a great journey for him—a journey that I would gladly help him complete.

I knew it was better for him to be deflated and *real* than to keep up the charade he'd kept up for so long.

The thing is, I've had this same conversation with dozens of friends and acquaintances in recent years. In fact, I'm guessing I could pull any random person out of almost any Starbucks line in the world, sit them down, and have nearly the same conversation with them, too.

Just as I'm pretty sure I could have a similar conversation with you.

Welcome to life in the modern world: a world in which most people have more wealth, knowledge, and technology (not to mention access to untold amounts of fresh-brewed coffee) than their ancestors could have ever dreamed for themselves. A world in which we have so much but so little. A world in which we seem to have it all, except for the ability to process it. A world in which we are constantly reaching for something, yet never seem to catch it—because we're not even sure what "it" is.

A world in which we are perpetually unsatisfied.

How bad have things become? The symptoms could hardly be more evident: The Centers for Disease Control and Prevention states that the prescribing of antidepressants has risen nearly 400 percent since 1988.[1] More than 10 percent of Americans over age 12 take an antidepressant.[2] That means more than one in 10 of us are taking a pill just to get through the day. And the fact is, more than 66 percent of severely depressed people aren't even included in that number, because they aren't taking antidepressants at all.[3]

Those are huge numbers, and yet I would argue that there are far more of us walking around with a feeling that makes those numbers seem small. There's a pervasive sense of malaise in the developed world—a sense of worry, of dread, of fear, of helplessness, of an inability to find the capacity to change or to feel better or to get out of our own way that all adds up to something bordering on, or perhaps even surpassing, what we colloquially define as depression.

So if you thought it was just you feeling this way, I hope there's some solace in knowing it's not. It's all of us. This problem is not just personal or communal—it's societal.

The world has developed so rapidly since the late 1980s that it seems impossible to take it all in. Our access to *everything* has exploded. Health and wealth have increased significantly. Meanwhile, crime and poverty, have decreased. According to every indicator, we should be overwhelmed with happiness. There is still pain and suffering in the world, of course, but compared to life 25 years ago, let alone a hundred or a thousand years ago, we are doing great.

So why are we less happy, less satisfied, more fed up, and far less enthused about our day-to-day existence than ever before?

WE ARE ENTERING A NEW ERA

Decades from now, we'll look back and recognize that this period we're in is one of the most transformative in human history—and you're a part of it, whether you like it or not.

We are in the midst of experiencing the shift to a digital age, a massive technological revolution that has transformed the way we interact with each other and the world around us. The fact that we have life-changing computing and telecommunications power in tiny devices that we carry in our pockets is incredible, but just as the Industrial Revolution brought all kinds of strife and challenge, this technological revolution is bringing new challenges with it as well.

In previous generations, wisdom was generally gained through a combination of hard work and time—whether that meant going to school or taking an apprenticeship or gaining years of experience simply by living and working in the brave new world. Now, information is available at every single moment and all at once. It's so much, so fast, that we can't possibly take it all in. What we're experiencing, then, is a breadth of information combined with a lack of depth. When we're able to access everything immediately, yet rarely get a chance to go deeper than the surface, that creates a massive problem. As the poet T.S. Eliot once said, "Where is the knowledge we have lost in information?"[4]

The superficiality of information is actually acting as an inoculation against wisdom. We *think* that we have all the knowledge we need when, in fact, we really don't. We're distracted all the time. We fall prey to the myth of multitasking (more on this in Chapter 12). When searching for knowledge, we'll read a quote or a maxim, hear someone's opinion and even gather a limited explanation but won't invest the time needed to fully understand any of it.

Think about this: Everywhere you look these days, you're bombarded by information that's designed to make you feel better. Feel-good Facebook memes, good-news websites and Twitter feeds, and self-help philosophies on positivity abound. You have access to all of it, 24/7 if you so desire. But is any of it truly making you feel better deep down where it counts? Even though the information offers some essential truth, I think most of us recognize that quick fixes and surface-level mantras don't work as a permanent solution. Even if they pick you up, there's always something that comes along and knocks you back down. And the more often that happens, whether you realize it or not, the more you begin to give up.

And *that* is what leaves us perpetually unsatisfied: when we think we've tried everything and read everything and seen everything, and we still don't feel good. So we give up on believing that we ever will.

Our need to find satisfaction in life is overwhelming. And in truth, finding that satisfaction comes from doing deep, real work. There is no quick fix for lasting contentment. Unlike getting a quick hit of happiness from a short-term distraction, true satisfaction requires investing a little more time and a little more effort into figuring out what's underneath all of these basic, intuitive bits of information that now flood our screens and our minds.

What we lack right now—and the thing that I aim to give you in these pages—is something that is fundamental to our existence: the ability to process your own life.

You already have all the ingredients for happiness, satisfaction and success. You do. We *all* do. The problem is that you don't know what to do with them. It's like having a refrigerator full of raw ingredients but not knowing how to cook. Staring at, discussing, and even touching the ingredients won't satisfy your hunger. It can't. It's not edible until you learn what to do with it.

And that hunger you feel in your life is not something small. That desire to be happy, fulfilled, and empowered—that desire is *existential*. That's why we all keep trying to get to it. You might think that hard work will get you there, so you work harder. You see other people smiling and assume they're satisfied, so you try to be like them. It doesn't work. And again, if you do that often enough, you're bound to give up and resign yourself to thinking you will never satisfy that hunger yourself. (That's why you're likely skeptical even as you read this.)

What if I told you that in order to get what you want, to achieve that sense of life satisfaction, all you need to do is change your relationship to what you already have? What if I told you there's a "golden lever" that allows you to bridge the gap between the life you have and the life you want? And all that is required in order for you to learn how to operate that lever is to understand yourself a little better—to read an operating manual, as it were, on how we actually function as human beings?

Well, it's true. The golden lever exists. I've spent my entire adult life in pursuit of it and in pursuit of the understanding of how that lever works. And guess what? I've found answers, most of which were right there in front of me the whole time. But as you'll soon learn, sometimes the things that are right in front of us are the hardest to see.

The fact is, most of us have failed to put in the work it takes to fully understand who we are. Most of us have no idea how to take advantage of all that life has to offer, because no one has showed us how.

That is what I would like to show you.

I suppose that leads us right back to the big question, the one that left my buddy Dave completely stumped: *What do you want?*

Truly, deep down, what is it that *you* want?

You don't have to answer that question quite yet. You need to learn a few things first so you can gain the wisdom that's needed to answer that question and then to understand how to implement the changes you seek.

So I hope you'll indulge me. I hope you'll be willing to invest a little time to take this journey with me. Because as you're about to see, not only are you capable of achieving the life you want, you are also capable—we *all* are capable—of all sorts of amazing things that at first seem, quite frankly, beyond belief.

PART I

HOW TO EXPERIENCE REALITY

CHAPTER 1

FAKE TESTS, OLD MEN, AND THE POWER OF BELIEFS

"Reality is merely an illusion,
albeit a very persistent one."

—ALBERT EINSTEIN

What you think about, you bring about."

Have you heard that phrase before? Or "What you believe, you will receive"?

We've all heard these maxims and others like them. They're memorable, catchy phrases. We're told that they're meaningful. In fact, there are people who put a lot of belief in these phrases, and some who proclaim that they have the power to work like spells— that if we think hard enough about winning the lottery, if we "believe it" enough, then we'll magically win the lottery.

Well, how many people do you know who wish they would win the lottery? Who dream about it? Who think about it *really hard*?

And how many of those people have actually won the lottery? Right.

There's no simple magic trick to bringing riches into your life. And yet, we are drawn to phrases like these, aren't we? Why do they hold such a prominent place in our minds and memories?

What if these phrases hint at a remarkable truth? Not in the immediate way we wish they would work. Not in some external fashion that allows us to control the world like we're wielding some kind of superpower. But in a manner that is internal, subtle, and, in some ways, far more powerful than most people would ever imagine.

OUR MINDS SHAPE REALITY

Let's begin at a small college in Boston called Harvard University. In the 1960s, a young psychology professor named Robert Rosenthal gained a reputation for thinking outside the box. Actually, for a decade or two, a lot of people thought that some of Rosenthal's theories were just plain crazy.[1] (Isn't this how breakthrough ideas seem to advance? As Albert Einstein said, "If at first the idea is not absurd, then there is no hope for it."[2] Breakthrough concepts are often counterintuitive and take time for the scientific community, let alone the general public, to accept.)

So, Rosenthal had this theory about the power and impact of the mind. He went to an elementary school in California, the Oak School,[3] with a new type of test that he said was designed to assess "blooming intelligence."[4] He claimed that with this test, he could identify which students would experience an intellectual growth spurt and outperform others in the upcoming school year, regardless of how they did in the past. He gave this test to all the students and then called in the teachers to share the results.

You could feel the palpable excitement as Rosenthal, the Harvard professor, read the names of the students who were going to have a breakthrough year.

But he left out one key detail: He'd made it all up. The test didn't actually predict anything. He just randomly chose the students, faked their scores, and pretended that those students were smarter than they were. (If you or I did that, we'd end up in jail, but guys from Harvard do it and they get tenure.)

The teachers went back to teaching, and Rosenthal left for the year. When he returned, he asked to review all the student test scores, and what he found nearly knocked him over. The students he'd randomly selected—the ones he told the teachers were about to bloom—had in fact risen to the top of their classes.

Can this be a coincidence? he wondered. Could he have randomly picked the smartest kids in the class? Lucky for him, he had added a little control to this experiment: In addition to his fake test, he had given the students an actual IQ test, and he knew which students had scored the highest.

Armed with that information, he decided to take his experiment to the next level. He gave all the students an IQ test again at year's end.

Have you ever taken an IQ test? You know, when that nice lady comes to your house to play blocks. Your mom is real nervous because she was told that they can tell how smart you are going to be for the rest of your life. She waits in the other room and then impatiently walks in and asks, "How did he do?" And the nice lady looks up says, "Uh . . . do you have any other kids?" (Okay, maybe that was just in my case.)

So Rosenthal gave these kids an IQ test, and it turns out the "blooming" students' IQs had actually gone up an average of 4 points higher than their peers—in a year! And in the youngest grade, the IQ differential was a high as 15 points.[5]

That led him to develop one of the greatest theories in psychology, called the Pygmalion Effect, or the Rosenthal Effect, which basically says this: Our minds don't just experience reality, they shape it.

The "blooming" students were not smarter than their peers. It was all made up! The teachers *mistakenly* thought these children were smarter than they actually were. It wasn't made public. It wasn't shared with parents. All that happened was that a teacher changed her belief about certain students, expected more from them, and likely altered, however subtly, how she treated them. The students subconsciously picked up on those expectations and adapted to them. They didn't become Einsteins overnight. They didn't cure cancer in the third grade. But they all accessed more of the potential they always had but for some reason couldn't reach.

Why? Because the mind shapes reality.

The vast majority of us have little appreciation for how powerful our minds really are. We think we know who we are and what we are capable of. We define ourselves as being "good at math" or "a people person" or "detailed oriented," and do not strive outside of those definitions. We build boxes that we fit ourselves into, and we extend that favor to everyone around us. We think we know our "reality."

What science is telling us is that we don't.[6]

CHAMBERMAIDS, PILOTS, AND THE FOUNTAIN OF YOUTH

Let's go back to Boston and meet another Harvard professor, Ellen Langer, PhD. The first female tenured faculty member in Harvard's psychology department, Langer has dedicated much of her career to pushing our understanding of the power of our brains. She has conducted experiments with such mind-blowing results that, once again, we're just starting to come to grips with them today.

In 1979, she created a study that was so incredible it became the basis for a television series in England—and has been replicated with strikingly similar results in diverse cultures such as South Korea.[7] Essentially, she pulled together a bunch of men in their 80s and took them on two separate retreats. Half of the guys went off to a peaceful setting at an old monastery in Peterborough, New Hampshire. For an entire week, they were cared for and treated with respect by a staff while they sat around *kvetching* about how old they felt. You can imagine the conversations about arthritis, their latest surgeries, and of course, the "good old days" when politicians never lied, people were hardworking, and kids were respectful.

The second group then went to the very same monastery, with the very same staff, but Dr. Langer treated them to something entirely different during their weeklong escape: She took them back in time.

She retrofitted the monastery to make it look and feel as if it were 1959, a full 20 years earlier. She instructed the participants to act as if it were 20 years earlier. There would be no talk about the present day; they had to act as if nothing that happened after 1959 had happened yet. They met daily to discuss "current events," such as "last year's" launch of the first U.S. satellite, *Explorer 1* (in 1958); they talked about the need for bomb shelters and Castro's advance into Havana; they got into heated discussions about communism; they recapped the Baltimore Colts' 31–16 defeat of the New York Giants in the NFL championship game; they watched Sgt. Bilko and Ed Sullivan on black-and-white televisions, and let Jack Benny and Jackie Gleason make them laugh.

At the start of the retreat, the men in both groups were tested for age-related symptoms: joint dexterity, memory, hair loss, arthritis, etc. She took photos of all of them, as well.

Almost immediately, Dr. Langer noticed changes. In both groups, the elderly men—many of whom were dependent on relatives or others who cared for them in their daily lives—were up and about, helping with chores, serving meals, and cleaning up after themselves. They all began functioning more independently. Simply changing their environments made a difference.

When the first group came back after spending a restful week remembering the good ol' days, there were some positive changes to their general health and well-being. Their hearing and memory were slightly improved. Their grips were stronger. The results can serve as scientific proof that a little independence can be a good thing, at any age.

But when the second group came back after experiencing their time warp, even Dr. Langer was blown away. In every single category, she found that these participants' age-related symptoms either stopped or *reversed*. They showed marked improvements to their intelligence, height, weight, gait, and posture. Their joints were more flexible, and their fingers even got longer (as the effects of arthritis were lessened and they could stretch out their fingers more fully).

Finally, she asked people unaware of the study's purpose to compare photos taken of the participants at the beginning and at the end of the vacation. These objective observers judged that all of the time-warp participants looked noticeably younger at the end of the study.

Dr. Langer's experiment showed the extent of how our minds shape reality. The students in the Oak School experiment were reacting to genuine expectations from their teachers. The teachers actually thought the students were smarter. In Langer's experiment, the participants knew it wasn't 1959; they knew it was all fabricated. But their surroundings painted a different picture. The minds of the elderly men picked up on the stimuli that suggested it was 20 years prior and sent signals throughout their bodies reflecting that "fact," which altered the aging process.

Dr. Langer decided to go further. She decided to focus in on a single physical attribute—vision—to see how our minds might impact our eyesight.

Most of us take it on faith that having 20/20 vision is an accurate measure of the biological reality of how well we can see. But how straightforward a measurement is it? After all, those eye charts in your optometrist's office are measuring not only the sharpness of the image on your eye's retina, but also your brain's interpretation of that information. So Dr. Langer posed a question: How much liberty does the interpreting mind take with this biological reality we call eyesight?

To find out, she recruited a group of students from Massachusetts Institute of Technology's ROTC program,[8] many of whom aspired to be pilots, and all of whom knew that good eyesight was a prerequisite.[9]

First, she tested their vision with standard eye charts. She then asked some of the volunteers to "become pilots" by flying in a flight simulator. She specifically instructed them to actively imagine themselves as pilots as they used the throttle, compass, and other trappings of an actual cockpit to execute flight maneuvers. They even wore green fatigues to enhance their role-playing.

No mention was made of vision to the "pilots" or to the control group, who merely sat in a stationary cockpit. After a short time, Dr. Langer surreptitiously measured the vision of all the volunteers. In the simulator, she had four aircraft "approach" from the front, each with a serial number on the wing. The volunteers were told to read these serial numbers. Unbeknownst to them, the serial numbers were written in the equivalent of different lines on an eye chart. She was in effect administering the optometrist's standard eye exam under the guise of flight simulation.

And what did she find? Unmistakably, those who were actively engaged in acting like pilots showed improvements in vision. Four of 10 volunteers could see better after playing pilot, compared to none of the members of the control group. Dr. Langer reran this experiment, in one case telling those in the control group they could motivate themselves to have better vision and in another case actually giving them eye exercises. But the "pilots" still outperformed them. In other words, by putting her test subjects into the position of acting like pilots—a group of people known to have good eyesight—she was able to sharpen the volunteer pilots' eyesight.

How is that possible? Isn't eyesight straightforward? Either you can or can't see something.

Well, no, it's not. Eyesight is processed through your mind, and when your mind anticipates not being able to see at a certain distance, you don't—even if you can.

Why? Because your mind shapes your reality.

A simpler experiment that shows the same results can be achieved just by flipping the sizes of the letters on the eye chart. Usually an eye chart has the big letters on top, and they get smaller as you look down. Dr. Langer and her researchers reversed the order and put the tiny letters up top, and guess what happened? People could see more of the smaller letters when they were placed near the top of the chart.[10] Why? Because as you look down the standard eye chart, your mind anticipates not being able to read some of the letters. Your mind doesn't have that limiting belief when the chart is flipped, so you can see more. Not everything, but *more*.

Your mind actually shapes your ability to *see*.

Dr. Langer went further, this time testing the ability of our minds to help us lose weight. Nearly three decades after her study on elderly men, she set up a health and fitness study with more than 80 chambermaids of various ages, chosen from seven carefully selected hotels.[11] At the outset, she asked all the women how much exercise they got. A third of them responded "none," and the other two-thirds responded that they did not work out regularly. These were all hardworking women putting in very long hours, so you can imagine their responses: "Exercise? What are you, joking? We're here early in the morning and work all day. Who has time to exercise?"

Dr. Langer took several measures of the women's basic fitness levels and then split them into two groups. The first group she dismissed, letting them go about their days as before. The second group, however, was given a presentation that showed just how much exercise they were getting from their jobs. She showed them that cleaning 15 rooms daily, pushing vacuum cleaners, scrubbing tubs, and pulling sheets actually constitutes more than enough activity to meet the accepted recommendation of a "healthy" daily half hour of physical activity. The researchers even provided specifics: 15 minutes of scrubbing burns 60 calories, 15 minutes of vacuuming burns 50 calories, etc. The basic message and the details were posted in the maids' lounges in the hotels where the second group of women worked, to serve as reminders, while the first group was left in the dark.

A month later, Dr. Langer checked back with the women. Every single woman in the second group—the group that had been told their daily work routine was, in fact, healthy "exercise"—lost weight. On average, the study's subjects lost 2 pounds, and their systolic blood pressure dropped by 10 points. They were "significantly healthier" by all measures. The women in the first group, however, those who were not taught that their daily tasks constituted exercise, saw no change in weight or health during that same period.

In surveys at the end of the study, none of the women reported any changes in behavior. No one had joined a gym. No one had made any big changes to their diets. They were all doing the same amount of cleaning. They were all doing the same amount of vacuuming. They were all making the same number of beds. *Nothing changed but their thoughts!*

That single mental shift changed their health.

So consider this: Right now, right this very second, your mind is shaping everything you do, everything you see and hear, and everything you think you know about reality.

And if your mind is shaping your reality, it begs one very important question: What is reality?

CHAPTER 2

JEAN PIAGET, THE FALLING TREE, AND THE SUPER BOWL CATCH

"We see only what is suggested by our thoughts."

THE TALMUD

Super Bowl XLII. Giants vs. Patriots. It was February 3, 2008, yet I remember it like it was yesterday.

The score is 14–10 Patriots, with one minute, fifteen seconds left to play.

The Giants have the ball on their own 44-yard line.

The 63,000-strong stadium rises to its feet in a wash of deafening noise, while millions of us all over the country ride the edge of our sofas in anticipation.

Let me give you some background. I come from New York, and New Yorkers have two principles in sports: love New York, hate Boston. It doesn't matter if it's the Giants and Patriots or the Yankees and Red Sox, it's bad blood. (Only sports-wise, of course. We love you, Boston!) But this wasn't just a game. This was the Super Bowl—the High Holidays of American sports. And despite the fact that the Pats came into that game undefeated and a 12-point favorite to win, my Giants were knockin' hard on Boston's door.

It was third down and five, and quarterback Eli Manning (of the Giants) was feeling the pressure. He escaped one tackle, spun away from another, and was finally forced to run from the pocket toward the sideline. Just when everyone thought the play (and the game) was over, Manning stopped and fired a pass across the field to David Tyree, who leaped in the air and made an unthinkable catch. First down!

The dozen or so guys around me jumped off the sofa in unison. You could feel it. This comeback was *happening.*

There was one guy in the room still sitting. He was a friend of mine who grew up in Boston. A die-hard Patriots fan. He looked sick to his stomach.

Four plays later, Manning found Plaxico Burress in the end zone for the go-ahead touchdown, and the Giants *won.* I just about lost my mind, as did every other New Yorker. You could hear shouts of joy echoing up and down streets from the Jersey Shore to eastern Long Island. It was beyond amazing. I'm not sure what heaven feels like, but I'm sure it's pretty close to how I was feeling that day.

In my excitement I looked over at my friend, the Patriots fan, and he looked like he'd just received word that he'd lost a family member. He was crushed. The color drained from his face.

I would go on to remember that day as one of the great days of my life; my friend would remember it as one of his worst.

The next morning, I had a thought: My friend and I were both sitting in the same room, watching the same event on the same television, at the exact same moment in time. We are both about the same age. We've known each other for more than 20 years. Our wives are friends. Our kids go to the same school. We were both living in the same "reality." So how could our experiences be so far apart? How could my experience be exhilarating while his was painful?

The answer may sound intuitive, even simple, but it's anything but. It has been the subject of discussion and debate among philosophers for generations and yet something that we rarely think about as we go about our lives.

The reason why my friend and I had vastly different feelings is because we each experienced a different version of reality. As close as we were in time and space, we each saw the game (and the world) through our own unique perspectives. We didn't experience the Super Bowl, we experienced our own individualized *perceptions* of the Super Bowl.

Our minds—filled with all of our beliefs, insecurities, habits, predispositions, prejudices, and preconceived notions—form a mental filter, and we experience life through that filter.

What separated the two of us in that game was not much more than a matter of geography: I was born in New York, and he was born in Boston. If my parents had lived four hours north, I'd remember that game totally differently. As a kid in Brooklyn, I was told that we root for the Giants, with our team colors and players. As a kid in Boston, he was told to root for the Patriots, with their team colors and players. We both brought our respective histories to game day, and those histories created the filters through which we experienced the same game in two very different ways.

This morning-after thought was about a lot more than football. This seemed to dig down to the root of how we experience *everything*.

We think we're experiencing reality.

We're not. What we experience is our *perception* of reality.

Every human being experiences their own version of reality, which they perceive through something called a "mental schema."

YOUR MENTAL SCHEMA

A mental schema is sort of like a pair of sunglasses through which everything you experience in life gets filtered. The concept of the schema was first introduced by the 18th-century philosopher Immanuel Kant[1] and later expanded on by researcher Jean Piaget, PhD, who studied children and their learning behaviors at the Grange-aux-Belles school for boys. Piaget adopted Kant's philosophical concept and made it relevant to psychology.[2]

One late night, as Piaget was grading papers, he noticed that children in different age groups were all getting similar questions wrong—in particular, those that required logical analysis or extrapolation from an experience. It was remarkable to him. It wasn't that any of these children suffered from an inability to learn certain material. The only difference between the students who were getting the answers to particular questions right and those who were getting them wrong was that they were in different stages of development, they had different life experiences, or they *lacked* certain life experiences, and that led them to think in certain ways and to therefore frame their answers differently.

Piaget decided to dig deeper, and by studying children at different ages and identifying the logic they used in order to answer certain types of questions, he came to the conclusion that all humans develop cognitive structures or frameworks through which they understand the world. These frameworks, these schemas, are not necessarily logical, and they vary from individual to individual. They are based on our knowledge, our experiences, and—importantly—our beliefs.

As we experience life, we create our own particular sunglasses—our schemas—by developing and adapting various cognitive structures with the information we gain and then store in our memories. The schema then provides us with mental shortcuts that are used to make future encounters with similar situations easier to navigate.[3]

As an example, your schema affects your commute to work: Once you go out and learn how to get to your office, your brain starts to learn how long it's going to take and which route to follow. After a few weeks, you don't have to consciously think about it. That's why sometimes we find ourselves at our desks in the morning without a clear recollection of how we got there.

The schema reminds us of who to be scared of and who to trust; who is friend and who is foe. Without a schema, we wouldn't be able to function, let alone succeed, in the world. We'd have to stop and relearn everything, all the time.

So how does your schema form?

When babies are born, they have very specific schemas. They interact with the world the only way they know how: through their mouths. As they grow older, they learn how to experience through other senses, and their mental structures adapt to their new ways of interacting with the world.

We all grow up the same way. We adapt to the stimuli around us. We make friends and learn what we need to do to gain social acceptance. We adopt religious and political beliefs. We choose careers.

Your schema is what you believe of the world.

Your schema is what you believe of yourself.

Your schema is the information you've built over your lifetime that is the filter through which you see the world. And because of that, your schema sets you up for different outcomes.

A kid who grows up in a supportive home may build a schema that says, "Taking risks is okay, because you're more valuable than any particular success or failure." So that person goes into life and looks at the world differently than someone who grew up in a home where they were always made to feel that they weren't good enough. It's not the *world* that's different for those two people; it's the same world. They're just wearing two different sets of sunglasses.

Well, what would happen if you could change your schema?

The fact is, for better or worse, whether you're choosing to do it or not, your schema is already in a process of evolving and changing—all the time. As experiences happen and new information is presented, new schemas are developed and old schemas are changed or modified through a process of what's called "accommodation" or "assimilation."[4]

Whenever the world around us meets our expectations, our schemas assimilate the information, reinforcing it in our minds. "I expected to be safe in my house and I was, so this is a safe place." "Everyone around me agrees with my opinions, so I know I'm right, and someone with a different viewpoint is wrong." Assimilation strengthens the memories and judgments and solidifies our schemas in those particular areas. When we are capable of predicting and explaining what happens to us, we are in a state of mental equilibrium, or cognitive balance. And that feels good. We want more of that. Without even thinking about it, we'll act in a way that leads us to that state of equilibrium—even if it's not good for us. Even if it's wrong.

On the other hand, when our expectations are met with disappointment, and our environment sends us stimulus that we don't want or that we've never encountered before, we enter into a state of *disequilibrium*. When any sort of new information cannot fit into our existing schemas, it creates an unpleasant feeling, and we seek to restore balance by a process called accommodation.[5]

Our best friend lied to us. We failed an exam we thought we aced. Someone introduced a fact that conflicts with our political views. In these moments, either we adapt our schemas to deal with the new information or we ignore it. Many of us choose to ignore it, even if only on a subconscious level, because changing our schemas is hard. Our natural tendency is to want to keep things as is. We'd do anything not to experience cognitive imbalance, even when it's good for us. Just ask someone addicted to a destructive behavior.

This desire to maintain cognitive equilibrium is deep-rooted, and our internal preference to focus on information that supports our schemas actually hampers the uptake of new information. This leads to stereotypes, biases, and prejudices.[6] We may not even realize it, but we'll remember certain information and overlook other information in an effort to maintain this equilibrium.

For example, if a businessman draws a knife on a homeless man, eyewitnesses may recount the episode incorrectly and say the homeless man was the one who pulled the knife. Why? Because our schemas have been trained to think that a man who lives on the street is more dangerous than a man who wears a suit. Such distortion of memory has been demonstrated through research on witness testimony. Witnesses to the very same incident will describe entirely different and contradictory "facts" about the same crime scene.[7]

Why?

Because we all see the world through different sunglasses, and therefore the very "facts" that we "witness" are altered by those glasses.

The schema shapes our theories about reality. And once we have these perceptions cast in our brains, they impact how new information is received. But this isn't just about what we see in the present; it impacts the past, as well.

What research has shown is that our long-term memories are neither fixed nor immutable, but are constantly being adjusted as our schemas evolve with experience. We construct our past in a process not unlike writing a book—a process of narrative. Much of what we "remember" is actually adjusted and rationalized to that narrative, so we can see our past as a continuous and coherent string of events, even though most likely it's not the case.

Everything—truly everything we consciously experience—passes through this mental schema we all have.

So the question is: Can we change our schemas the same way we can change a pair of sunglasses? And if so, can we purposefully change our schemas in a way that will make our lives better?

THE FALLEN TREE

We all want a better life. In fact, I think it's safe to say that we all want a *great* life. How one defines "great" will vary from person to person, of course, but what drives us, what excites us and worries us when we really drill down on it, is the pursuit of a quality life experience.

What we've been taught—through society, through our education systems, through almost everything we see and hear—is that our circumstances determine the quality of our lives. "Your life will get better once you get that new job." "You'll finally be content once you settle down and get married." "You'll feel confident once you lose all that weight." "I'd be so much happier if I moved someplace warm!"

The thing is, it doesn't add up. Great circumstances don't automatically lead to a great life. We see it all around us: successful entrepreneurs and CEOs who climb to the top of the business world and still feel "empty"; actors, singers, and other celebrities who've turned to drugs and alcohol to chase away their demons after acquiring all the riches and fame they thought they wanted; your next-door neighbor or colleague or family member who seems to have everything but is always complaining.

More importantly, it's within your own life's story. You've had great moments. Maybe you scored the winning goal or got an A on the big test. Maybe you landed that great job or fell in love. Maybe you bought a new home or moved to a new city. Whatever it is, it felt good for a while. But then the excitement wore off. The new house started to feel like your old house, with a few more rooms. You got into the college of your dreams only to realize that you just replaced the academic rat race of high school with a similar one, adding no more clarity of its relevance to your life. The game, the test, the relationship somehow started to lose its glow.

We spend the vast majority of our lives pursuing circumstances, assuming that as soon as we achieve them, we'll experience what a "great life" feels like. But even when we succeed, after the initial high, it still doesn't feel like we've arrived.

What if we have it wrong?

What if circumstances aren't causative to experience but merely correlative? Meaning, what if what happens to you doesn't automatically lead to how you feel? What if circumstances are a factor—maybe a big factor—in your experience, but there is a missing piece, a component, a cog in the wheel that is more directly connected to how you feel and how you experience life?

What if what's making you feel satisfied or unsatisfied is less about what's going on around you and more about how you process it all?

What if the way to have a great life is to first master how to *experience* life? What if only then can you understand what it is you want to achieve and accomplish?

What science has shown is that everything that happens to you only gets experienced once it is processed through your mind. Which means the work you do to improve your life needs to be focused on not just what goes on outside of you, but most importantly how it all gets processed inside of you—because your mind is shaping your reality.

Everything that happens around us is neutral. *It is our minds that create the meaning.*

Let's piggyback off the famous philosophical question, "If a tree falls in a forest and no one is around to hear it, does it make a sound?" This question has been the subject of both philosophical and scientific debate for centuries and speaks to the heart of what we are discussing: namely, the nature of reality. But I want to focus this just on us and *our* perception of reality.

The falling of a tree is a neutral event; it is our minds that interpret that event for us to experience. Depending on your schema, you may cry at that tree's falling, recognizing it as a home to the animals that used it for shelter. You may see that tree representing something much larger: a time when nature was preserved and left untouched by ambitious human hands. You may see it as a positive improvement, as the area in which the tree stood is being developed for urban use that will lead to growth in population and commerce. You may see it as one of a billion trees and not care one bit. Or you may never know it, as the news of its falling will never reach your consciousness.

There are thousands of possibilities for the interpretation of one tree falling, and nearly every person who looks at that one neutral event will see it differently. And all of it will likely change in an hour, a day, or a decade after the event.

Everything in life is that way. It is not the circumstance but the mind that creates the experience.

Sitting in traffic can be the worst thing in the world, the thing that raises your blood pressure and leads to your heart attack in 10 years; or it can be the most peaceful part of your entire day, when you get to listen to music or escape to another world through an audiobook, uninterrupted by your kids. Traveling by plane can be stressful and miserable, or it can be a welcome opportunity to take a break from everyday life, fly through the air, and see a different part of the world.

Think of any circumstance in life and you'll quickly see it's possible to experience that circumstance in multiple ways. Experiences depend almost entirely on the interpretation of our minds through the filter of our schemas.

Learning how to change your mental schema isn't easy. It takes active effort. But once you see the possibility of it, once you fully get it, there is no turning back. And it is so immensely worth it.

Your life experience will change—because it *can*.

The answer to what you want in life isn't "out there." It's in your mind. It's in *you*. It's found in your ability to learn how to process life in an entirely new way.

MEET RAQUEL

I had just wrapped up a long day of speaking at a corporate seminar in Los Angeles when I first met Raquel. She approached me that late afternoon in search of some personalized advice, and I could tell right away that she was in a bad place. She was in her early 50s, brunette, a nice-looking woman, but she seemed to be hiding behind a bit of a fake smile. I could tell that she was fighting to hold back tears as she attempted to get her words out.

"Would you mind if I tell you my story?" she said.

We sat down as people were still milling around the hall, yet the background noise seemed to fade away as Raquel told me about her divorce.

She and her husband had married young. He'd built a successful career as a partner at a large law firm, and together they'd raised a handful of beautiful children, who were now all moved out of the house. So after 27 years of marriage, she was shocked when her husband came to her and said things weren't working out.

"Now that the kids are grown," he told her, he realized that he "didn't have that feeling for her" anymore. He'd kept it together for the sake of the children, but now he felt it was time to move on.

She was devastated. She was completely lost without him. Her whole *world* was this man and the family they had built together.

Then it got worse. A year later, after the divorce was finalized, he announced that he was not only dating but planning to marry his colleague—a beautiful woman 20 years Raquel's junior.

At first, the kids rallied around Mom. In a sense, that new dynamic became her life: Dad was the guy who everyone hated, and she wrapped herself in the love and support of her children. But after a while, the kids started to forgive him. After all, he was their dad. And once that happened, the kids stopped wanting to hear their mom complain about how "bad" he was. In time, they not only began to accept him and his new life, but they accepted his fiancée, too.

Raquel was beside herself. Not only had her husband sold her out, but now it felt like her kids were selling her out. She became bitter. It was all-consuming. Every single conversation she had with friends and family became about *that*. She admitted she'd also become paranoid. When the kids didn't immediately text or call her back, she assumed it was a sign that they were siding with *him*.

As she sat in front of me, it was clear that she was stuck in a spiral of bitterness, guilt, pain, and confusion. She absolutely could not forgive her husband for what he did to her—but she knew that she'd lose her family if she didn't.

I started by asking her what she thought about the idea that our minds shape reality. She said it made sense to her. So I asked if she could see how her feelings, however justified, were really just based on her schema—her particular view of what she felt she deserved from others.

She nodded. "Sure," she said.

"So, then you understand that if you change how you see things," I said, "if you change your point of view on all of this, if you change your schema to start filtering things in a new way, it will change how you feel. And *that* will change how you act and what you talk about every time the kids call. Changing your perception is really what's needed in order to start reversing this spiral."

Her response was, "Wow, that sounds great." I felt happy that she got it—until she completed her thought. "That sounds great," she said, "if I was a robot."

She wasn't having it.

"It's all fine and dandy if I could just plug it into the system, like I was a computer, but there's no way that can happen," she said. "I'm a human being. I'm emotional! I can't just 'change my thinking.'"

Ah. Now that's the rub, isn't it?

If we truly believed that "What you think about, you bring about," we wouldn't question our ability to make the changes we seek in ourselves. But most of us hold on to a set of big doubts about the power of our minds to hold any sway over our emotions, let alone anything else.

The pain and suffering we feel as a result of whatever horrible circumstance has unfolded is just the way it is—it's "reality," we think—and because we can't change it, we need to learn to live within it.

I realized that my journey with Raquel was just beginning. At that point, at that table, on that late afternoon, she didn't have the knowledge or tools she needed in order to heal. It struck me that although she was in a totally different place in her life, she wasn't all that different from my friend Dave. He hadn't gone through a divorce, he didn't have grown children, he wasn't grappling with that same pain of betrayal, yet he also lacked the practical wisdom he needed in order to change the things he listed as "wrong" in his life.

Neither Dave nor Raquel understood that they already held the power to alter their schemas, to change the very thoughts and beliefs that were coloring everything they experienced and therefore to change their realities—because neither of them understood the full, magnificent power of their own brains.

What they (and, frankly, most people) were missing was a basic understanding of the most breakthrough scientific concepts to emerge in the last hundred years: the discovery that the human brain is ready, willing, and, most importantly, *able* to change itself—and I mean *physically change itself*—at any time, at any age.

How?

Through the miracle of neuroplasticity.

CHAPTER 3

THE POWER OF PLASTICITY: CAN WE FUNCTION WITH HALF A BRAIN?

"Your brain is a work in progress. From the day we're born to the day we die, it continuously revises and remodels, improving or slowly declining, as a function of how we use it."

—MICHAEL MERZENICH, AWARD-WINNING NEUROSCIENTIST
AND LEADING AUTHORITY ON NEUROPLASTICITY

There's a man who can see through his tongue.

Not through his eyes. Through his tongue.

Rajesh Malik has been blind since birth. Because of an underdevelopment of his optic nerves, he cannot see form, distance, or another human being.[1]

He has led a great life anyway, never letting his disability hold him back. He believes he can do things any seeing person can do, and he has done that: He became a husband and a father, and he earned his doctorate in personality psychology.

Beliefs are powerful.

But Rajesh had one particular dream that seemed impossible to fulfill: He wanted to play ball with his kids. That simple interaction between parents and their children eluded him. He tried, but the best he could hope for was to hear a ball bounce off the wall behind him or to hear the sound of one of his children's voices guiding him to find the ball on the floor.

That changed one day when his doctor, Maurice Ptito, PhD, a neuroscientist with a lab near Rajesh's home in Montreal, invited him to try on a device called a BrainPort.

What is a BrainPort? Let's go back 30 years to meet its creator, Paul Bach-y-Rita, MD, a neuroscientist and chair of Rehabilitation Medicine at the University of Wisconsin. After his father suffered a debilitating stroke, Dr. Bach-y-Rita started to study the power of the brain in an effort to rehabilitate his father. What he uncovered was a radically new way to see the brain and its incredible ability to change and re-create itself, a science called neuroplasticity.

He began testing the limits of sensory substitution. We've all heard that blind people develop a better sense of smell, right? The notion is that when one sense is damaged, the brain can adapt to deal with new stimuli by making the other senses more sensitive and acute. But Dr. Bach-y-Rita wondered, could one part of the body *substitute* for the other? Could the body and its touch receptors "take over" for the eyes and act as a substitute retina, enabling blind people to see?

Dr. Bach-y-Rita believed that we see with our brains and not our eyes. So all the brain would have to do is take tactile information and convert it into visual information. Sound impossible?

Breakthrough ideas typically do. Lucky for us, he didn't let it stop his curiosity. In the end, his hypothesis proved true.

Dr. Bach-y-Rita developed a device that routed visual images to electrodes taped to the skin on people's backs. In his experiments, his patients sat in an electrically stimulated chair that had a large camera behind it. The camera scanned the area and sent electrical signals of the image to hundreds of vibrating stimulators on the patient's back. It worked. His blind subjects could "see" the images that the camera picked up *through their backs*.

Years later, he discovered that the tongue, being much more sensitive than most skin areas, was an even better conduit for delivering substitute senses. So he built a machine he called the BrainPort, which looked like a hard hat with a camera mounted to it, connected by electrodes to a small tongue depressor.

Back to Rajesh. Under the guidance of Dr. Ptito, Rajesh put on the BrainPort and placed the tongue depressor in his mouth. The machine's cameras scanned the images in front of Rajesh and sent signals through the wires of the depressor onto Rajesh's tongue.

Within seconds, Rajesh Malik—a man who had been blind since birth and who had no memory of sight to draw upon—began to *see*. Through the stimulation of his tongue, he saw shapes. Objects. Obstacles placed in his way. He could reach his hand out and pick an object up. It was as if his brain had been ready and waiting to see. It knew what to do. It just needed a new way to get that information. Once the stimuli were delivered, his brain adapted—instantly disregarding the fact that Rajesh's eyes didn't function.

With a little practice using this new "sight," Rajesh was able to walk through a maze without bumping into walls. More importantly to him, he learned to see the shape of a soccer ball rolling toward him and to figure out from the visual cues when to swing his foot out so he could kick it.

Through the help of some breakthrough science, Rajesh was

finally able to do what he wanted most: play ball with his kids.

Recently, the FDA approved a smaller, lighter version of the BrainPort (with a tiny camera affixed to the center of a pair of sunglasses) for market in the United States.[2] As more people learn about it, more improvements are made, and the price of the technology comes down, the blind may be able to experience life in a way they never imagined.

How is this possible?

How could the brain adapt itself to see through the *tongue*?

Because our brains are adaptable. Our brains are changeable. They are capable of far more impressive feats than we've given them credit for in all of human history. And it's only recently that scientists have even begun to understand just how much power exists in that gray matter in between our ears.

OUR POWERFUL BRAIN

Most of us have no idea how our brains work. Why would we? We're not brain surgeons or neuroscientists. Who has the time or capacity to sit and study voluminous textbooks on the science of that 3-pound mass in our skulls. Even if we did, do scientific textbooks tell us what is in our minds? They may show how the brain functions or where to perform surgery if a specific part is not functioning properly, but what I'm talking about is the inner workings of your mind. There's no one else who can figure that out but *you*. Your brain is your point of access to everything in your life. It's the conduit to what you see and do and touch and feel and experience in this world.

And yet we walk around every day, going about our routines, with little idea how to work the mental operating system that connects us to life itself. We don't appreciate the full extent of its capabilities. In fact, I think most of us assume that the brain controls *us* more than we control *it*.

If you don't have the life you want, maybe it's not because something is wrong with you or something is missing or you aren't working hard enough. Maybe it's simply because you haven't slowed down enough to understand your resources and learn about the controls at your disposal. Your brain is like a complicated dashboard. You have switches within your reach that either no one has shown you or you simply don't know how to use. You have access to a control system through which you can alter the trajectory of your life—if you just knew how.

THE MIRACLE OF NEUROPLASTICITY

Has anyone ever told you that you can't learn new things after a certain age? If you're an adult, mastering a new language, learning how to play piano, or excelling at a new profession are supposedly out of reach.

"You can't teach an old dog new tricks."

When an idea has reached the level of a catchphrase, it must be true, right?

No. It's not.

Age isn't the only thing that supposedly limits our brains, of course—it's this sense that intelligence is something that is fixed when we are born. It's "common knowledge" that each of us is born with a certain amount of intellectual capacity and, to quote every mom who speaks English, "You get what you get, and you don't get upset."

The development of the IQ test was the proof of this. We've been told that we can take a test and get a score that is the numerical measure of our baseline of intelligence. Whatever number the IQ examiner gives you is the number you're stuck with, for life.

Only that's not true, either.

Alfred Binet, the inventor of the Binet IQ test, said that the notion that our intelligence is fixed is pure bunk. In his book,

Modern Ideas about Children, he states: "We must protest and react against this brutal pessimism. With practice, training, and above all, method, we manage to increase our attention, our memory, our judgment and literally become more intelligent than we were before."[3]

So Binet—the creator of the test that we believed could tell us how smart we will be for the rest of our lives—said no one can tell you how smart you will be for the rest of your life. Each of us has the ability to impact how intelligent we will be.

Part of the reason we haven't heard much about this is because our understanding of neuroplasticity is all very new. For centuries, scientists thought the brain was machinelike: hardwired and fixed into place. It was only in the late 1990s when researchers began seriously exploring the miraculous truth about the human brain: that our brains are endlessly adaptable, malleable, and reshapable; and that our thoughts have the power to reshape the physical structure of our brains. *Plastic* is the term scientists use to describe that quality, and this new field of study—this breakthrough field that has the power to change everything in all of our lives—is called neuroplasticity. Neuroplasticity posits that our brains are always shifting, always changing, *always growing* based on our thoughts.[4]

Why is this important to you and me? Because neuroplasticity is the pathway to understanding why we do what we do and how to change it.

Leading neuroscientist Norman Doidge, MD, believes these findings are nothing short of a revolution. He states in his best-selling book, *The Brain That Changes Itself*: The "idea that the brain can change its own structure and function through thought and activity is . . . the most important alteration in our view of the brain since we first sketched out its basic anatomy and the workings of its basic component, the neuron."[5]

We already knew that our brains were incredibly powerful

machines. Back when we thought that our brains were fixed, they were still ridiculously impressive. The brain is made up of approximately 100 billion neurons.[6] Each neuron has somewhere between 1,000 and 10,000 synapses, equaling about 1 quadrillion synapses.[7] Those neurons, connected by synapses, are joined into vast networks that process low-level electrical currents that fly through our heads at speeds up to 200 miles per hour.[8]

What we didn't know until very recently was that our thoughts have the power to literally change the physical structure of our own brains.

This isn't just new scientific ground for academics to ponder at MIT or Columbia University. This is the sort of stuff that should constantly be making headlines. We're on the forefront of an entirely new understanding of life here, and it's exciting. It's the next frontier of scientific breakthrough, and it will change the way we see ourselves and each other. The discussion of "neuroplasticity" is so frequent in my household that my kids roll their eyes at me before I even utter the word. They know when I'm going to say it because I say it all the time. Anyone who listens to my speeches or radio show has heard the word a thousand times, too, but the fact is, the broader population isn't aware of this field yet and has no clue about the power it holds to change our lives. To be living at the forefront of the understanding of neuroplasticity is as big as living at the dawn of a nationwide railroad system before anyone laid down a single track.

It changes *everything*.

The fact that Rajesh Malik can see through his tongue is just one example of the extreme lengths our brains can go to in order to accomplish seemingly impossible tasks. The brain is so flexible that it can create new neuropathways to bypass missing nerves.

Our "normal" nervous system has volumes of information that pass through it in a particular way. Should there be a block or a defect or some inability for the brain to get the information as it typically does, we used to assume that such a breakdown caused a permanent loss of that functionality. Victims of strokes, head injuries, and birth defects were conditioned to live within their limitations.

But neuroplasticity has changed all that. For such "victims" today, all hope is not lost. The brain has a capacity to rewire that information through a different route and still maintain some part of that functionality—not unlike the way a modern GPS mapping program can give a driver multiple routes to reach a destination.

NEUROPLASTICITY EXPLAINED

What the study of neuroplasticity tells us is that the brain changes itself and adapts itself through one remarkable channel: our thoughts.

There are billions of neurons in our minds, forming complex neural maps that enable us to function as human beings. Some of these neurons were interconnected from birth, enabling us to survive. No one has to teach a newborn to breathe or cry or suck. They are born with those skills and have the corresponding neural connections to go with it.

There are, however, neurons that are not connected. Those neurons depend on our experiences in order to get connected. How do they do that? Through thought. Thoughts connect neurons to each other, remapping our brain to adapt to new knowledge, language, and skills as we navigate through life.

For those who are interested in the finer science of it, here's an oversimplification of a super-complex process. Neurons are separated by a space called the synaptic cleft. They exchange information by sending electrical or chemical messages, or neurotransmitters, across the synapse. When one neuron connects to another, it triggers an electrical impulse that causes the neuron to "fire." As neurons fire repeatedly, molecular alterations occur in both of them and their relationship strengthens. Their connection grows stronger, and they eventually become wired together.

This concept, introduced by famed Canadian neuropsychologist Donald Hebb, is known as Hebb's Law, and it's summed up by the phrase, "Neurons that fire together, wire together."[9]

So when you have certain thoughts, a neuron gets connected to another neuron. The more you reinforce those thoughts, the stronger those connections get. So the simple act of thinking either makes new connections or fortifies your existing ones.

To help make sense of it, let's take that concept all the way back to childhood.

The reason I can look at a round object and say "ball" isn't because I was born gifted in the English language. It's because when I was little and pointed to the round object in my room, my parents said "ball." So I repeated "ball." At that moment, my brain created a thin neurological connection between the object and the word *ball*. Since I grew up around people speaking English, the word and the object were reinforced so many times that now in my brain, there is a rock-solid connection. If you woke me up in the middle of the night and showed me a basketball and asked if I knew what it was, I would not hesitate. I wouldn't have to Google it. I would automatically say "ball."

On the other hand, if I thought about something just once or twice and then stopped thinking about it, the neuroconnection would start to weaken and eventually disappear. That's why it is possible to forget certain words entirely. That's also why we do not remember most of what we learned in high school. Unless those subjects are part of your career or personal interests, chances are you haven't interacted with that information since you passed your final exam. I know that if you were to give me a periodic table today, I would be lost. I would probably be able to find the *O* for oxygen and the *H* for hydrogen (maybe), but that's it. It's not because I am handicapped at chemistry (although my sophomore year grades may have indicated that possibility), it's because I haven't looked at anything remotely close to chemistry since then. My brain, after forming a thin connection to the periodic table, dissolved it.

This process is called "synaptic pruning."[10] Think of your brain like an experienced gardener. Every day, it plants new seeds and prunes the weeds. In fact, the success of any garden is not only in the growth of healthy plants, it's in the removal of the dead ones.

Your brain is constantly creating and removing neurological connections. It creates new neurological connections when information is introduced. When we learn, study, and challenge our minds, those neurological connections become stronger and our intellectual capacity grows. However, it also looks for unused neuroconnections to fade away. Consequently, if we stop being exposed to certain kinds of information, these connections will weaken and even disappear.

So why should all of this matter to you?

Because neuroplasticity is the ticket to getting to the life you want.

The fact that you can literally change the structure of your brain—just through thoughts—is the ultimate game changer. If our minds shape reality and our schemas determine our quality of life, then neuroplasticity is both permission and proof that each of us has the ability to enhance, modify, and transform not only our minds, but also our lives.

THE WOMAN WHO CHANGED HER BRAIN

Barbara Arrowsmith is a model of neuroplasticity.[11] At an early age, she was told she was disabled, different, even "stupid." Her educators pointed out that her brain did not work the way it was supposed to. Arrowsmith couldn't so much as tell time. The simple face of a clock made no sense to her, no matter how many times her parents or teachers tried to explain it. She couldn't understand basic cause-and-effect relationships—in other words, why things would happen from moment to moment. She couldn't understand human relationships, either, and was unable to reconcile how one woman could be both her aunt and her mother's sister at the same time. She also suffered physical ailments, including poor motor control and inaccurate sensitivities on the entire left side of her body, which made her a danger to herself. Language and reading were nearly impossible. Life seemed to come at her in fragmented bits and pieces.

She was diagnosed with dyslexia and dyscalculia. Because of the severity of her learning disabilities—which included spatial reasoning, logic, and kinesthetic perception—the general assumption was that she would never function normally and was advised to "learn to live within her limitations."[12]

As she did her best to progress through school and into adolescence, everything got harder. Her ability to read progressed a bit over time, and yet she found that she couldn't understand the words on the page of even an introductory philosophy book. The relationships of concrete subjects were confusing enough. The relationships of abstract concepts on a page were simply baffling. She would have to read papers and reports sometimes 20 times before they would make any sense at all.

Finally, just before high school, she resigned herself to the idea that life was never going to get better. She tried to take her own life—and, as she says, felt ashamed when she woke up the next morning, unable to complete even that task with any success.[13]

Thankfully, her father, an inventor and scientist, taught her a couple of valuable lessons in life. First, if there's a problem and no apparent solution, it's up to you to create a solution. And second, in order to solve a problem, you have to identify its core components.

So Arrowsmith decided to go on a lifelong quest: to understand the reason for her challenges. She focused on finishing high school and then went on to college, where she studied psychology. Then at the age of 26 she read a book called *The Man with a Shattered World* by Russian neuropsychologist Aleksandr Luria.[14] The book was filled with research on a Russian soldier, Lyova Zazetsky, who had been shot in combat and wound up with a bullet lodged in one small portion of his brain. It turned out that Zazetsky's symptoms were uncannily similar to her own, right down to the inability to tell time. As she read the book, it occurred to her that her brain wasn't "disabled"; instead, one particular portion of her brain was *damaged*.

With that new knowledge in hand, she started to research what eventually would become known as neuroplasticity (in particular the work of American researcher Mark Rosenzweig and his research on laboratory rats[15]). What she soon realized was that by studying the information in a different way, she might be able to "fix" that portion of her brain.

She laid out daily exercises for studying clocks, trying to establish the relationship between the two hands on the face of the clock as a way to teach her brain, forcefully, that relationships—any relationships—actually exist at all. She labored relentlessly at retraining her brain. She spent hours practicing, working with self-created flash cards and putting together drills she created to help with memorization (studying pictures, poems, and more). She practiced daily, without fail. And then something happened. One day, she looked at a clock and was able to tell time. It made sense to her.

But that wasn't all. Something near miraculous happened after that: She walked into a library, pulled a philosophy book off the shelf, opened to a random page, and read it. And what she read made sense to her—*on the very first try*.[16]

She wondered if it was a fluke. Maybe it was just an easy book.

She kept pulling books off the shelves, opening to random pages, and repeating her trial. She wound up surrounded by a dozen books and understood each one of them.

Emboldened by these results, she decided to create exercises to strengthen her brain in lots of other ways. She eventually overcame the sensation and motor-control problems on the left side of her body and much, much more.

"I was living proof of human neuroplasticity," she declared in her widely viewed TED Talk.[17] And she's right. She is proof that it is entirely possible to overcome even severe problems in the human brain, simply through stimulating thought.

Arrowsmith isn't superhuman. According to society's preconceived (and, frankly, inaccurate) notions, she was severely "disabled" because of this injured part of her brain. She was starting at a disadvantage, and yet look at what she achieved. She launched her own study center and has written books, given TED Talks, and inspired thousands of people to push past their perceived limitations.

Arrowsmith could have adopted the schema of her educators, who tried to lower her expectations and convince her that she was permanently disabled. Had she adopted that schema, she would have looked at the world through the prism of her limitations. But beliefs are powerful, and the mind shapes reality. Arrowsmith's refusal to give in or give up changed her life. She approached her education through new angles. She saw solutions that were "invisible" to others. She created new ways to get information to her brain through the use of exercises that "typical" students didn't need.

Her schema enabled her to innovate new methods of learning, which, once she understood the information, created new neuro connections and pathways. These gave her both the content and the skills she was lacking, enabling her to overcome what others perceived as her "disability."

It's staggering to think about how much of our lives are unrealized, not because of our lack of capacity, but because of our limiting beliefs. Maybe the problems we are facing require new solutions—new methods, angles, and approaches to pursue. Maybe the people we rely on don't have all the answers and we have a lot more to contribute, to innovate, than we would have otherwise imagined. By realizing that maximizing our potential lies, in part, in how we see ourselves and how we see what's possible, we can take the first step on a path to creating stronger, more resilient beliefs, enhancing our schemas, and searching for ways to create new neurological pathways to overcome the obstacles that stand in our way.[18]

FUNCTIONING WITH HALF A BRAIN

The example of Barbara Arrowsmith is not a solitary one. In fact, there are examples of neuroplasticity in action that are even more (dare I say it) mind-blowing.

Michelle Mack lost functioning of the left side of her brain during a pre-birth stroke, yet the right side of her brain made up for it. Growing up was difficult for her, but thanks to a can-do attitude, she can now speak normally, she graduated from high school, and she has a job. She has her challenges but is living what most people would describe as a functional, typical life—with half a brain![19]

Finley Rosbotham was born with cerebral palsy and was physically missing nearly half of his brain at birth. His twin sister was healthy, though, and as she grew and started to crawl, so did he. His doctors said he would never be able to walk. But he has. With time, exercise, and practice, his parents (and sister) have been able to help train the right side of his brain to master functioning that normally would have been taken care of by his brain's missing piece.

Neuroplasticity is so reliably powerful that doctors now regularly perform a radical surgery called a hemispherectomy, the removal of one half of the brain. The surgery, first developed in the 1930s and later revived by Dr. Ben Carson in the 1980s, is used as a cure to eliminate seizures caused by Rasmussen's encephalitis, a rare degenerative inflammatory neurological disease.[20] By 2008, Johns Hopkins was doing six of these surgeries a year, and what doctors have found is that thanks to the brain's incredible plasticity, there are few long-term side effects on brain function or IQ from the surgery. After one side of the brain is removed, the other side has the ability to make up for the functioning of what is lost, and the body fills the empty gap with fluid. Many patients have gone on to live normal healthy lives with no significant impact on their memory, personality, or general cognitive capacity.[21]

Let me just say that again: People who have lost half of their brains live with minimal effects on how their brain functions.

As Dr. Carson said, "Human beings are incredible creatures with a brain that is beyond belief in terms of its capabilities. To the point where we can take half of it out and it can still function in a normal way."[22]

It kind of makes you wonder what people with healthy, functioning brains are capable of, doesn't it?

While these and other sensational stories of neuroplasticity may occasionally make the news or your Facebook newsfeed, the stories you're less likely to hear are more subtle: the one of the woman who suffered a devastating loss of a loved one and restructured her brain in a way that allowed her to get back on her feet and find happiness again; or the guy who was able to lose weight simply by changing his *thoughts* about food and exercise. These stories aren't making noise, but that's how people use neuroplasticity to shift the course of their everyday lives.

How far can we take this? Let's think about how we deal with pain. Pain is all brain function. Or how we deal with addiction—that's brain function, too.

Simply knowing that we can deliberately and purposefully restructure our brains means that the methods and approaches to how we deal with life's challenges can change.

All thoughts affect the brain. In a way, thoughts affect the brain as much as drugs do. Thoughts may take longer to have an impact, but their ultimate effect is more precise and harder to erase.

THE PROBLEMS OF PLASTICITY

Of course, there are potential negative effects as well. Neuroplasticity is also the reason we suffer from some of the behaviors that drag us down and hold us back in life. Since your brain gets its material from your life experience, when something goes wrong, it adapts for that deficiency.

Dr. Doidge explains: "Neuroplasticity isn't all good news; it renders our brains not only more resourceful but also more vulnerable to outside influences. . . . Ironically, some of our most stubborn habits and disorders are products of our plasticity. . . . It is by understanding both the positive and negative effects of plasticity that we can truly understand the extent of human possibilities."[23]

For example, if you've expressed your love for somebody and been rejected, you may have learned to stop being vulnerable in future relationships. If you've launched a project or company and wound up embarrassed by failure, you may adopt a greater fear of taking risks. If you turn to drugs or alcohol or food every time something goes wrong in your life, it will become harder and harder to *not* do that if things go wrong again (which they always do).

The brain puts up certain blocks, creates certain traps, and sets up automatic responses to protect itself. As a result, we can lose the ability to "run the software" properly. Unless we are investigating the holes in our system, we run the risk of repeating our ineffective ways and getting the same poor results in life no matter what happens.

There is an old expression that "knowledge is power." That expression is not entirely true. *Empowering* knowledge is power, yes. But destructive knowledge is debilitating. Our fears and insecurities, negative behaviors, and destructive habits are reinforced actions that are neurologically programmed in our minds. That's why we find ourselves struggling with the same issues year after year. It's because how we deal with life's challenges becomes deeply ingrained in who we are.

When we just complain about our problems, when we give up in the face of challenge, we reinforce that response in our minds. Our brains strengthen those neuroconnections, which create a schema with more negativity and weakness. Over time, it gets harder to deal with similar circumstances in a productive manner. We feel weaker, and as the cycle of negativity gets "faster" (since it occurs with more mental ease), we become more incapable. Our minds are shaping our realities.

So neuroplasticity is a powerful tool that must be wielded thoughtfully, mindfully, as it were. Remember that phrase "What you think about, you bring about"? This is closer to how it actually works. When we understand it and use it correctly, though, it's one of the greatest gifts we have. Neuroplasticity tells us that the stuff that's "wrong" with us doesn't have to stay wrong forever. The things we do, the way we think, the compulsions we have are merely neurological pathways that have been created in our brains, in some cases without our consent or knowledge. And our neurological pathways can be changed if we choose to put in the effort to change them.

CREATING DISTANCE

In order to begin to change your life, it's important to acknowledge this crucial bit of information: Your brain is not *you*. It's a part of you—it's the dashboard of your life—but it's not *you*. Change begins when you place a chasm, however small, between you and your brain.

Think about it like this: When you go to the gym to work out, you do so under the assumption that you have muscles, right? "You" are not your biceps. You *have* biceps and can grow them or let them weaken. The existential distance you place between "you" and your muscles is what enables you to attempt to change them. While the distance between you and your brain is harder to realize, since it's in your head and you can't see it, it's just as critical.

You are not your brain. You *have* a brain.

Your brain is a supercomputer that you can alter (through neuroplasticity) much in the way that you alter your muscles—not through physical exercise, but through mental exercise. Therefore, the negative or limiting neurological pathways in your brain do not define you. They are a part of your brain that, if you want, you can replace or upgrade.

What's the difference between you and other people who seem more successful in life than you? When you look at truly successful people, what they have in common is their mentality. They created and maintained deep neurological connections that led them to their achievements. If an external circumstance takes away their money, job, or even a loved one, they somehow seem to be able to rebuild and reemerge as they once were. It's not luck or circumstance. You assume they're just *destined* for success, when the truth is that their minds are *programmed* for success. More accurately, their thoughts have programmed their minds for success. And our minds shape reality.

Your life is based on your neurological programming. What

goes into your mind—or, more precisely, what your schema allows into your mind—shapes your brain.

So if your life isn't where you want it to be—if your life isn't "great"—the reason for that may be nothing more than you've created neurological patterns that are leading you down the wrong road.

Isn't it time you started creating neuropathways to greatness instead?

How? By understanding the limits of your attention.

CHAPTER 4

SEEING MINIVANS AND MISSING REALITY: THE SURPRISING VALUE OF LIMITED ATTENTION

"Man can alter his life by altering his thinking."

—WILLIAM JAMES,
KNOWN AS "THE FATHER OF AMERICAN PSYCHOLOGY"

I married young. I had my oldest son at 22 and then, at 25, my wife gave birth to twin girls. After our initial elation over having two more babies at once waned a bit, we realized that my midsize Nissan Altima was not going to be big enough to hold our family.

So one morning, over a cup of coffee, my wife casually said to me, "I think we should get a minivan."

I knew this was coming. I was prepared.

"Honey," I began, "I don't think we can get a minivan. It's not that I don't want to, I do. Who wouldn't want a car whose number one feature is the amount of cup holders? It's just that I am in my twenties, and I don't want to be the first guy in the universe to drive a minivan in his twenties. I'm not ready for that level of leadership in the larger minivan community."

"No problem," she said. "Let's just go to the dealership and figure out what to get once we're there."

I should have seen it coming. There was no way I was going to walk into a dealership and outplay the joint effort of a leasing agent and a mom with three kids under the age of 3. I didn't stand a chance.

So, as we drove off the lot in our brand-new minivan, I tried to save face. "Honey," I said, "I'm so happy we got the minivan, but I am just too young to completely surrender my manhood. How about this: I won't drive this around the neighborhood. You can be the one to drive it locally. I'll just drive on road trips."

"No problem," she said.

You see where this is going.

So that night, as I drove our new minivan through our neighborhood on my way to go pick up diapers, I stopped at a red light. I looked to my left, and in the very next lane was a guy who looked just my age—driving a minivan!

I honked the horn and motioned him to roll down his window. He did.

"Nice minivan!" I said, all enthused. "You look good it in!" I was so happy to see the second-ever twentysomething-year-old guy in a minivan.

He gave me a strange look and slowly turned his head as his window rolled up.

I came home and told my wife, "You'll never believe it. There was another guy my age in a minivan!" She paused and asked, "How did we end up together again?"

In the days that followed, I started to see them everywhere. (Okay, not *everywhere*, but more than nowhere.)

Why had I never noticed?

Here's why: Our brains are limited in one very significant way: in how much information they process at any given time.

The schema is the filter through which we see the world. Our experiences, beliefs, and neuroplasticity all make up the contents of our schemas, and it is through that prism, those sunglasses, that we see our "reality." But the schema does more than just paint the color of what we experience; it actually determines whether we experience it at all.

There are millions of stimuli around us, all the time, but we simply cannot process them all. In fact our nervous systems can only process approximately 110 bits of information per second.[1] That's it. That's all we get.

If I'm standing in front of a classroom and speaking, in order for you to hear me and understand what I'm saying, you need to process about 60 bits of information per second.[2] You're also processing other stimuli around you at the same time: checking the clock, feeling hot or cold, catching glimpses of other people in your peripheral vision, tapping your pencil on the table. All of that little stuff takes up processing power, too. And if one other person starts talking at the same time, requiring another 60 bits per second, you're suddenly overloaded. That's why you can't understand two people talking to you at the same time. Science gives us the explanation as to why your mother yelled "One at a time!" when you and your brother started talking over one another at the dinner table.

At any given moment, you're processing all sorts of things you aren't even aware of. You may be eating or drinking. You may be hearing the rain outside or people talking in the distance. The way your brain processes stimuli without being overloaded is by choosing which stimuli to focus on. It determines what's most important to stay focused on and doesn't process the rest.

In fractions of a second, your brain decides whether certain stimuli are important or not, and it simply blocks out the unimportant ones. Those rejected stimuli never make it past your filter. Do they exist? Sure. But you don't know it because you haven't experienced it.[3]

How does the schema know what's important? It looks for information for which we have context. So if we have no knowledge about something, or no experience from which to draw, it will—as Piaget saw in his students—miss the information entirely.

Before I bought my minivan, minivans simply weren't a part of my life. Were there young guys in minivans all over the place? Absolutely. But my particular life experience formed my mental filter, my schema, which did not include young dads driving minivans—and so, for me, they didn't exist. I'm sure you've had plenty of similar experiences in your life, too. It could be a make or model of car that you'd never noticed until you bought one yourself. It could be a word you never knew but now seemed to show up in every book you read. It could be an annoying motorized fan running in the back of one of your appliances that you'd never heard before but now seems louder than anything else in the room.

What this tells us is that in any given moment, there are all sorts of things going on around us that we aren't aware of that may be affecting our lives. It means that the way we've shaped our personal sunglasses—our schemas—determines not only how we process the information we receive but also whether or not we receive the information in the first place. This is important, because what we turn our attention to is what enters our consciousness, and the number of things we can pay attention to at any given time is extremely limited.

As William James, MD, known as the father of American psychology, said, "Millions of items of the outward order are present to my senses which never properly enter into my experience. Why? Because they have no interest for me. My experience is what I agree to attend to. Only those items which I notice shape my mind."[4]

That's why the idea of effective multitasking is mostly inaccurate. You only have a limited amount of capacity to interpret information, so if you're doing two or three things at once, you can only give a small portion of your attention to each task. We're all aware of this when we talk to someone on the phone: If they're scrolling through Twitter or answering e-mails while you're talking to them, you know it. You know they're distracted and aren't giving you their full attention, simply because they aren't making the normal sorts of responses and cues we've come to expect during an engaged conversation.

Productive people don't multitask. Instead, they give all their attention to whatever task is in front of them, and then put all their attention into the next task and the next, without overlap. We see this in athletes who are on their game, businesswomen who are in a zone during a speech, surgeons who are in the middle of a lifesaving surgery. They're not texting, tweeting, or scrolling. They are fully focused. Their entire mental allocation is focused on the task at hand, which is what makes them more likely to succeed.[5]

The thing is, for most people, life happens *to* them. They experience what is put in front of them. Their beliefs and their perspectives are shaped by whatever events happen to them. They don't choose where to place their attention. It's chosen for them. They just passively experience it.

But top performers aren't passive at all. They take the reins. They learn how to control what they experience, what they believe, and what they perceive. That enables them to change their experiences *and* their circumstances.

Again, think about great athletes, businesspeople, doctors—those who climb to the top of the ladder of their particular fields.

How do they do what they do?

Through focus.

CONTROLLING YOUR FOCUS

Let's go back to Raquel's story for a moment, the woman struggling with life as a divorcee. Through the process of attending a seminar and talking one-on-one, she gained a pretty good grasp of the information you've now read about in these opening chapters. She came to grips with the idea that our minds shape reality. She seemed to get the concept that reality is perceived through our schemas. And she also began to grasp the concept of neuroplasticity—that the mind is constantly regenerating itself and that our thoughts hold the extraordinary ability to change the physical structure of our brains.

What none of that taught her is *how* to gain control of her life, *how* to change her life, or *how* to become a happier person.

To Raquel's point, we're not robots. So how do we force ourselves to stop thinking the thoughts that are in our minds? If every time we have a thought it creates stronger neuroplasticity, and we can't control our thoughts, how can we change? I'm not a Jedi Master. I'm guessing you're not, either.

Neither you nor I nor anyone else has the power to just stop our thoughts—of anger, regret, doubt, bitterness, or any others that seem to get in our way. So isn't that the brick wall in the way of our progress? If neuroplasticity is true, then every time I have a negative thought, every time I think I'm ugly, I'm a failure, "she hurt me," or whatever, it's only going to get worse. Those thoughts create and reinforce themselves in neuropathways that are harder and harder for our brains to "prune out." Therefore, I keep bringing myself further down a path that I don't want to walk down.

So what's the solution?

Focus.

We'll get to this in a big way later in this book, but the answer starts with the fact that we can focus only on a limited number of things at any given time. And you have more control over what those are than you think.

Picture a city filled with activity, so much of which is impossible to control internally. But you can assert control from the outside if you control the border, the access to and from the city.

Your mind has millions of neurons firing at every moment. Memories, emotions, automatic responses are being processed every nanosecond. You can't control all of that. But the information that gets to your consciousness comes in through a small bridge, your attention—a finite amount of stimulus you can process at any given moment. The key to changing your life is taking back that bridge. With conscious effort, you can take that limited window, the 110 bits of information per second, and force your plastic brain to create or reinforce empowering neurological connections.

SHIFTING GEARS

Let's climb back into the minivan for a moment. Actually, it doesn't matter what kind of car it is, so let's make it a Ferrari. (Hey, I need to get back in touch with my manliness.)

When you're zipping down the road in your Ferrari, you'll pass hundreds of cars without actually being aware of them. Their shapes and colors might register for a fraction of a second, but they'll all be immediately forgotten. They don't require any of your real attention.

However, if a car is swerving unsteadily in front of you, you immediately focus additional attention on it. You register the visual image of the car and relate it to a memory of other errant cars to fit it into certain categories: *Is the driver inexperienced? Drunk? Distracted?*

You note the color. You note the movements.

Then you evaluate: *Should I worry? Should I act? Speed up, slow down, change lanes, stop, dial 911 to alert the highway patrol?*

All of these complex mental operations happen in a few seconds, and they happen through a shift in attention. A shift in focus.

Attention selects relevant bits of information from the potential millions of bits available and then retrieves appropriate references from memory, to evaluate and then act. Attention is limited, and increased attention in one area limits attention in others. After noticing the swerving car, you'll likely stop talking on the phone or singing along to the radio if you want to avoid an accident.[6]

That's control. Your ability to focus attention on something specific for as long as it takes to achieve a goal.

In moments of perceived danger, we do it automatically. But why do we have to wait for a crisis? We have the ability to focus our attention whenever and wherever we want. Through attention, we can direct our minds and change our thoughts and feelings.

"Geniuses," as William James explained, "are commonly believed to excel other men in their power of sustained attention."[7]

THE POWER OF DISTRACTION

So how do we do it? How do we change our focus away from the negative aspects of our lives?

Every parent already knows.

When a child falls on the floor, what do parents do? First, they clean them up and make sure nothing is broken. But the child is likely still crying with no signs of letting up.

What do parents do to calm them down? Reason with them? Nope. Beg, plead, lecture, or discipline them? Not going to work.

How do they get them to stop crying? They distract them. They make a joke, blame the floor (ever try that one?), or promise them ice cream. (It's amazing how much parenting is based on sugar consumption.)

They change their child's focus. Why? Because when their attention moves to something besides the pain, they actually feel the pain less.

Learning to shift focus isn't just about distraction. It's a way to create new neuroplasticity. When you shift your focus from something that's negative to something that's positive, and you do it again and again, thanks to neuroplasticity, you make it easier to focus on the positive, instinctively.

Identifying what we want and need to focus on will be covered extensively later on in this book, but let me give you three examples of how shifting focus can change how you feel.

If you're married and your marriage is not amazing (assuming that both you and your spouse are not bad people and you want your marriage to work), try the following: When you look at your spouse, think about what you're focused on. Is it what's wrong with him or her? Are you thinking about the times he annoyed you, the way she disappointed you, the expectations you had for marriage that have not been realized in your life? As you look at your spouse and continuously focus on what is wrong, what you're doing is developing a picture that is negative or disappointing. As a result, that feeling of disappointment translates into how you interact. That disappointment poisons your schema's "view" of your marriage.

So for one week, try something new. Whenever you're frustrated, just shift your focus. When you look at your spouse, identify the five best qualities about him or her. When he's disappointing you, is he still trying? If so, focus on the trying. Focus on the positive effort. Better still, go back to the reasons you got married and try to see those things in him, separate from the pressures of raising children, finances, or anything else that's dragging your marriage down. For one week, try to consistently focus on the positive traits of your spouse. Force yourself to think about them. Shift your attention to those positive traits, over and over again. Force your brain to see those positive traits.

Even if this feels unnatural at first, you will start to change your schema. You will start to see the positive more easily and therefore feel more positive about your spouse and about your marriage. That will let you feel happier just to be around him, and that will ultimately translate into how you feel about him and how the marriage develops.[8]

Another example: happiness. Years ago, a mentor of mine told me, "Every morning when you wake up, write down four things that you're grateful for. Spend just one minute thinking about your life without those things and then being grateful for them." Your eyesight. Your hearing. Your ability to walk. Living in a home. Living in a secure environment. Having the ability to support yourself. Having a family. Whatever it may be, you have lots to be grateful for.

But here's the trick, he said: You can never repeat any of the things on your list. For the first week, it's pretty easy to come up with that list. But after that week, it takes effort. You have to find things that you've never taken the time to be grateful for in the past. And so you train your brain to look for things to be grateful for throughout your day. You start seeing them and taking note of them: that you didn't miss the bus, that your digestive system can break down foods, that your immune system kept you from getting sick this winter.

When you train yourself to look for four things to be grateful for every day, in time you'll find yourself feeling happier. Why? Because when you're looking for things to be grateful for, you are shifting your attention, however slightly, to becoming more positive about your world and about your life, which your mind then translates to feeling happier. All it takes is that shift in where you're focusing your attention.

At your job, you've probably known the feeling of giving a presentation or finalizing a project and getting all sorts of positive comments, but then one person criticizes you and that's all you can think about for the rest of the day. Why? Because it stands out in our minds. Because we're self-conscious. When you think about that criticism, it reinforces the neuroplasticity in your mind that's been built around feelings of "I'm not good enough."

Here's how you change it: As soon as someone gives you a compliment, stop whatever you're doing and focus on that compliment with greater attention than you normally would. In fact, start to focus your attention on *all* of the positive responses you received, and you'll find that gradually, over time, you'll start to gravitate toward thinking about what you did right, rather than obsessing over what you did wrong. And that allows you to build on your strengths rather than be held down by your weaknesses.

When you spend time shifting your attention, even just a little bit, you're able to change how you feel and therefore change how you experience life.

You've probably heard the phrase "Where your focus goes, your energy flows."[9] It's so commonly used in everything from self-help books to massage manuals that it's become cliché. But why? Why do these types of phrases stick? Because just like the phrase "What you think about, you bring about," this phrase contains an essential truth.

Where you place your focus changes everything. Changing your focus changes your ability to see, hear, feel, and experience what's right in front of you, in every way—from minivans to love to signs of danger, to potential opportunities, even to happiness itself.

What I explained to Raquel was that in order for her to change how she felt, she didn't need to change her *thoughts*. She just needed to change her *focus*. She needed to focus on new things in her life in order to change her way of seeing the world. And that's what we got started on right away.

WHAT ARE WE MISSING?

Have you thought about where your focus and attention are right now?

What if you're filtering out all of the good things in your life—including your potential—by using up your limited processing power by focusing on negative things? What if you're assuming you can only have a mediocre career when you can actually have an incredible one? What if you're assuming you can only have an average marriage when you can have an amazing one?

If you believe that you can't, then your mind will prove you right. When you change your focus, you can change your beliefs and your schema—and you may well find that the opportunities you are looking for are right before your eyes. What you'll find is that you were just blind to them before, the same way I was blind to seeing young guys driving minivans.

The relationships you are dreaming of, the power and courage you see in others but not yourself, the financial opportunities you thought always passed you by—all of these things are there. They exist. You just haven't been able to see them.

What we know through studies on perception, beliefs, and neuroplasticity is that if you believe you are not enough, you will make it true. If you believe that you are incapable, unworthy, or unloved, your mind will find a way to prove it.

But what happens when you believe that you *are* worthy? What if you believe that you *are* capable? What if you believe that you have the power to make a difference in the world, to be happy, to be an incredible parent, to fully love your spouse? If you believe it, your perspective changes. Your perception of reality shows you a brighter tomorrow, and your mind looks for a way to make it possible.

If you are living an unhappy life, it means that your schema is off. You have a filter to see negative, and your confirmation bias and natural inclination to fight against cognitive dissonance are bringing that reality into fruition.

I am not, in any way, suggesting to gloss over the challenges you have or ignore the people or circumstances that bring you pain. But if you want the strength to deal with difficult times, you need to start by taking more control over your attention and ability to shift your focus. When you focus on people who will help you instead of hurt you; when you focus on stimuli that will make you feel empowered and not hopeless, then you'll start to change your schema. And you will automatically start to develop a new world of neuroplasticity that will change how you do, see, feel, and experience everything that life has to offer.

THE 10,000-HOUR RULE

It's usually around this point when someone wants to see some results, immediately. We're all a little impatient these days, aren't we? I understand the need for speed. This is exciting stuff. And we've been hindered in this high-speed digital age without an understanding of just how to process it all.

So, let's get to it: How long does it take to reprogram the brain? How many hours or days or weeks or years will it take for you to see a tangible change in your life?

I'm sorry to say that science has not uncovered a concrete answer. Retraining the brain seems to vary from person to person, task to task. In fact, there are only two real insights we have when it comes to figuring out how long it takes to make a significant shift in the brain, and those insights live at opposite ends of the time spectrum.

The first is a little something that's entered the vernacular in recent years: the 10,000-hour rule. This finding has been popularized by Malcolm Gladwell in his bestselling book, *Outliers*.[10] In it, he describes how studies have shown that it takes a person about 10,000 hours of concentrated time and practice in order to "master" a particular skill. The effect of this rule is seen in people we generally think of as "masters"—concert pianists, world-class athletes, chess masters, even "master" criminals. He goes on to explain that even those people we call prodigies, who seem to accomplish so much at such a young age, have just put in their 10,000 hours of practice while the rest of us were out playing in the dirt or watching cartoons.

So if 10,000 hours is required to reprogram our brains, it's pretty discouraging, right? Most of us can't dedicate 12 hours a day to concentrating on any one thing. We're lucky if we can spend an hour a day in any sort of concentrated task. And waiting years to see change is a hard sell in today's world.

The good news is that most changes we seek to make and "master" within ourselves take far fewer hours to accomplish. (I'll share more specifics about this in Part III.) In fact, neuroplasticity is triggered every time you think, so your brain is always changing and adapting—however undetectable—based on your thoughts. In many cases, you can see changes soon after you start to learn a new skill or increase your brain activity in any one particular area.

THE *TETRIS* EFFECT

Remember the video game *Tetris*? It's a computer game where you fit shapes together, like mini puzzle pieces falling from the sky, and when you put together a solid row of shapes, the lines at the bottom of the screen disappear, making room for more pieces. Of course you gain points along the way. Fun game. Addictive.

The game was first developed by an artificial intelligence scientist named Alexey Pajitnov.[11]

In 1991, Richard Haier, PhD, of the University of California at Irvine's Department of Psychology used *Tetris* in a series of brain studies. By scanning the brains of college students while they played the game, he saw something pretty remarkable: The scans of players who were new to the game lit up with all sorts of brain activity as the players figured out how to conquer this new task. However, after days of playing the game for even an hour or two at a time, the brain scans stopped lighting up. The amount of brain activity required in order to play the game went down.[12]

This was actually a rather early glimpse of neuroplasticity at work. Once the brain learned how to play the game, it created new, appropriate neuropathways. So as the player moved up in levels and the game got harder, the brain was able to adapt and adjust in the most efficient way possible.

More than a decade later, Dr. Haier did another study on adolescent girls who played *Tetris* for an average of 90 minutes per week over the course of 3 months. What he found was that the girls' cerebral cortex (the place in our brains where the neuroconnections happen)[13] grew thicker over those weeks, signaling an increase in connections formed, while brain activity in other areas *decreased*.

He concluded, "[W]e think the brain is learning which areas not to use. . . . As you learn the game, it becomes more automatic."[14]

Dr. Haier's 2009 study further demonstrated that when you do specific tasks over and over again, they take up *less* of your brainpower over time. And remember: These students weren't playing the game 12 hours a day. Their brains changed physically by dedicating just 90 minutes a week.

The amazing thing the study showed is that change happened in the brain over a very short period of time. The rewiring of the brain happened almost immediately. It may take time to establish world-class expertise—if you were interested in becoming an expert in *Tetris*, you may have to play for hundreds and hundreds of hours—but the study showed that neuroconnections were created as soon as the player focused in on playing the game.

Dr. Haier's experiments show that our brains are working every moment. When you shift your attention, when you change what you focus on, you can immediately begin wiring your brain in a new and improved way.

You can put these same processes to work for whatever goal you seek: to find happiness, achieve success, and even to live a more fulfilling life.

THE BIG QUESTION

The tools of focus and control are what you need to begin changing your experiences for the better. But before we can implement any change, there is still a big question you have to answer.

It's the same big question that baffled my friend Dave; the same question that Raquel needed to answer before she could heal and move forward in her post-divorce life.

What do you want?

Actually, let's add another word to that question, just to drive it home:

What do you *really* want?

You don't have to answer now. Chances are, even if you think you know the answer, you probably don't. Not the real answer, anyway.

And that's okay.

What we're about to delve into will help you to answer that big question, once and for all.

PART II

HOW TO SATISFY OUR NEEDS

CHAPTER 5

DECONSTRUCTING DESIRE: DO YOU WANT IT OR DO YOU *NEED* IT?

"I can control my passions and emotions if I can understand their nature."

—BARUCH SPINOZA,
17TH-CENTURY PHILOSOPHER

It's the question we ask our 5-year-old when he's in the middle of a temper tantrum. It's the question we ask the moody teenager when she's moping around the house. It's the question we ask our middle-age friend at Starbucks, the one who seems to have everything but feels he has nothing:

What do you want?

How can we go about our lives every day and not know the answer to that question? Oh, sure, maybe you're able to spout off some pat answer like, "I want to be happy!" or "I want to be rich and famous!" or, if you're my 10-year-old, "I want an iPad!" But let's face it: Most of us have no real clarity about what will bring us the highest level of satisfaction and fulfillment in life.

We keep moving along, assuming we'll feel what we want once we get it.

But have we taken the time to really ponder the big question, let alone think about the myriad questions that go along with it? "What drives you?" "What do you consider a good day?" "What do you consider a bad day?" "Why are certain moments considered a 'success' and others a 'failure'?" "What are you working toward?"

If we don't try to understand what we want, how can we ever expect to achieve it?

Our minds are supercomputers. We know that. We've seen it. And we've barely begun to understand just how immense the brain's capabilities are. But the one thing it cannot do is direct itself. Our military can build fleets of $100 million F-35A stealth fighter jets, but all of that cutting-edge technology is useless without trained pilots.

Our brains need an operator. They need to be directed where to go. And in order to take control of your brain, in order to gain control of your life, you need to understand what you want.

The first step in that journey is to pull back and take a look at your desires.

DECONSTRUCTING DESIRE

Desire is at the core of our existence. It's what creates context to guide our lives. Desire isn't a bad thing; it's the most powerful feeling we have. Without desire, we would never get out of bed, we would not muster the strength to overcome challenges or engage in that daily grind, and we would certainly not have the motivation to push our lives in the direction in which we want it to go.

Every day, you wake up with desires. You desire food. You desire money. You desire to see your loved one. You desire to get to the gym, or you desire to watch the latest episode of your favorite show.

How do you fulfill a desire?

Let's start with an easy one: the desire to eat. Your mind goes back to your neuroprogramming, and asks, "What did I do beforehand?" The answer it finds is not that you went outside and harvested your crops or hunted a deer in order to eat. The answer is most likely, "I went to the kitchen and looked in the refrigerator" or "I went to my favorite coffee shop." So when you wake up in the morning and you're hungry, you're going to go do something similar to fulfill that hunger.

So "desire" is really this: An underlying need (in this case hunger) coupled with our memory of a past experience of how we fulfilled that need (in this case going to the kitchen or the coffee shop), melded with the expectation or anticipation that we will fulfill that need in the same way again (there will be food in the fridge and muffins at the shop).

To express it a little differently, here's a simple formula we can use:

$$Desire = Need + Experience + Expectation$$

The first needs any of us know in life are physical. When we're born, we have a need for oxygen, so we breathe; we have a need for nourishment, so we suck; we have a need to understand

and connect, so we use our senses to explore the world around us; and so on.

Since we started life consciously aware of only physical needs, we are programmed from the start to think that satisfying these needs is the entirety of our goals in life.

We know that due to neuroplasticity, long-term, repeated programming is hard to shake. So as we go through life, it's easier for us to stay primarily focused on satisfying our material needs, which, in most cases, is to the exclusion of our deeper, more innate needs.

The pursuit of material needs—the things we can touch, taste, see, smell, etc.—is not just neurologically favored because it was our primary focus in the early stages of our lives. Materialism has specific components that make it more likely to create and reinforce neuroconnections than loftier ones. I call this the Trap of Materialism, because in order to appreciate the dominance of materialism on our lives, we need to see how it impacts our minds.

THE TRAP OF MATERIALISM

There are three reasons why materialism causes such strong plasticity. First, material pursuits are largely sensory. Sensory experiences create strong neuroconnections, especially when mixed with dopamine, the neurotransmitter released by the brain as a response to pleasure. When engaged in physical pleasures, you are not only forming new neuroconnections—those connections are being cemented together with dopamine.[1]

Eat a bag of M&Ms, and that heightened physical sensation of super-concentrated sugars on your tongue is sure to leave an impression. Once a neuroconnection is made and cemented with dopamine, it takes time and effort for the brain to prune it away. That's one reason why sugary foods are so hard to resist.[2]

Second, material pursuits are, by their very nature, limited. They only last as long as you're engaged in them. Because they don't offer any lingering pleasure, they create an anticipation in us to reengage in the activity. Potato chips taste great until you finish the last chip, and then they're gone. You want more chips because you want that sensation again, and it only lasts for as long as you're physically eating them. The same can be said of thrill-seeking, like riding a roller coaster or cliff-diving. The sensation fades, and if you liked the sensation, you'll find yourself craving it again. The same, for some people, can be said of shopping trips to the mall.

Lastly, in order to achieve the same level of satisfaction, material pursuits always need *more*. As the neuroconnections grow stronger, the pleasure becomes familiar and less exciting. As a result, you need more of it in quantity and quality just to maintain the same baseline of satisfaction.

Examples of this are found in addictions to drugs and alcohol, where the fix needs to get bigger and bigger over time. But it happens in all facets of our lives, and the cycle never ends—because fulfilling your material desires alone cannot ever fully satisfy you.

Material pursuits don't make us happy or fulfilled. One quick look at the long list of Hollywood's tragic fallen stars proves it.

We assume that our lack of satisfaction is coming from the lack of physical objects and sensations. But it's not. Our feeling of lacking in life is not because we don't have enough materialism, it's because we spend too much of our time in pursuit of it.

NEEDS VS. WANTS

When we spend most of our time in pursuit of materialism, we wind up not being able to distinguish between what we need and what we want.

Have you ever walked through a toy store with a 5-year-old? You know, when your kid grabs a toy off the shelf and starts to carry it to the front of the store without asking?

"Put that back, honey," you say.

"No!" the child protests. "I need it! I need it!"

I feel like I've spent half of my adult life trying to explain to my children that most of what they ask for they don't actually *need*, they just *want*. Sometimes I feel like I should spend the rest of my life explaining this very same thing to adults.

Needs are essentials; wants are luxuries. Distinguishing between a need and a want is one of the hardest things we can do. It requires us to reprogram how we see things. When we were little, everything seemed like a need. We didn't want new sneakers, we needed them. We didn't want to win the game, we needed to win. And as we got older, most of us never upgraded our thinking. We still look at the world and see needs when most things are wants.

Here's the difference: A want comes from a place of abundance; it is additive to our lives, and we won't suffer a fundamental negative impact should we not get it. Needs are deeper. Needs involve our very survival, whether it's physical, emotional, or spiritual in nature. Hence, if we don't fulfill our needs, that lack of fulfillment threatens our mental health, our emotional well-being, or our very existence.

Do I *need* a new toy? A new car? A new job title? A bigger house? The answer to all of those questions is probably no. You can live without any of those things. You don't actually need them. They all fall under the category of wants. But when we live as if we *do* need them, then we feel a lack without them. We create an expectation that once we get them, we will feel satisfied. We think the object of our desires will fill the hole we feel in our lives.

Only it doesn't. Since none of those objects fulfill actual needs, they don't restore any of the lack you're feeling. You don't feel satisfied. You just wind up wanting more, thinking that you still *need* more in order to feel complete.

So no matter how important it is to you to maintain a certain lifestyle, get the latest gadget, or experience that vacation, all of those things are fundamentally wants. You need to have some money to put food on the table; you want to have a certain level of income to afford expensive items. It's not wrong to have wants— everyone does, and it's a major motivating force in life. But it's critical to understand that there is a difference.

In order to feel satisfaction with the *wants*, what you need to do first is try to satisfy your *needs*. And that means you have to identify what those needs are.

OBJECTS OF OUR DESIRE

Let's go back to our formula for a second and take a closer look:

$$\text{Desire} = \text{Need} + \text{Experience} + \text{Expectation}$$

Desires in life are not, by definition, "needs." They are expressions of needs, coupled with experience and expectation. Our desires are actually our wants. However, you do not desire (or want) a particular thing *just because*; you want it because you're attempting to satisfy a deeper need.

The confusion arises when we assume that the only way to satisfy a need is through a particular want; that a specific object is the only path to meet our deeper needs. Why would we think that? Because our previous experience tells us so. Remember what Jean Piaget discovered about his students: They answered questions based on their experiences or lack thereof.

When you look out to the world to satisfy your needs, your schema sees what it knows. It looks for the objects that it is familiar with. It pulls an experience, a memory, and concludes that the only way to satisfy a need is with that particular want. But what if it's wrong? What if there are myriad ways to satisfy our needs that we never even considered? What if there are minivans that we never saw? What if there are all sorts of opportunities that have simply been invisible to us?

If our schemas are based on our experiences, then for the most part, they are shaped, not by us, but by the world around us. Our experiences are influenced by the media; by our schools and communities; by our hundreds of "friends" on our social platforms; by a system that thrives on our consumption of goods and services. What if the pursuit of nearly every desire we have was influenced and directed by everyone around us and not us?

Think about it: Why do you want to get into that university? Why do you want that career? When you dream of "success," what picture pops into your mind, and why? Why are you so interested in a relationship with that person? Why are you affiliated with a particular way of thinking or political group? Your needs are the underlying force that is within you, but maybe the destinations you want have been chosen for you.

The greatest block to personal success in life is not a lack of resources, it is a lack of clarity. Understanding what we want is important, but first we should understand why we want it. Our desires present a window into our needs, and that is where we have to look to find the answers for what's missing in our lives. Then, and only then, can we start working toward bridging the gap and truly achieving the life we want.

OUR INNATE NEEDS

Identifying our desires and using them as a path to discover our needs is not a new idea. In fact, it's been the focus of the career of famed researcher Edward Deci, PhD.

Dr. Deci began his career in Rochester, New York, studying people's desire to engage in puzzles and thought-provoking games—crossword puzzles, Sudoku, things like that. Not only did he want to know why people find it so satisfying to solve puzzles, but he also attempted to understand the differences in people's attitudes, concentration levels, and skill levels when they're trying to complete puzzles on their own versus when they've been motivated for monetary or other external rewards. Deci started to develop a theory about what it takes for people to tap into their "intrinsic motivation."[3]

What he found is that when people engage in activities that satisfy their "innate needs" as human beings, they feel an intrinsic desire to do that activity. That left him asking: What are these innate needs?

It would take Dr. Deci a couple of decades to find the answers. While working with Richard Ryan, PhD, he identified three psychological needs that exist not just in people who love to do crossword puzzles, but in every one of us. Those needs are:

1. Competence
2. Relatedness
3. Autonomy

What Drs. Deci and Ryan found is that these needs are like the psychological nutrients of our lives, and when we engage these needs, when we access and satisfy them, we feel more fulfilled.

These three needs would combine to become known as the Self-Determination Theory[4]—an all-encompassing theory that explains why we do what we do. This theory gives us a clue about how to make ourselves feel whole. Figure out how to fill these innate needs and we will feel different. We will feel more alive. We will feel empowered.

So what exactly are these needs?

Competence is a need to control the outcome of situations and to experience mastery, which means we want to feel capable of building, doing, accomplishing, and achieving. (This is the need that drives people to want to complete puzzles, solve mysteries, finish projects, etc.)

Relatedness is the need to interact, to be connected to and experience caring for others. Our actions and daily activities involve other people, and through this we seek a deeply necessary feeling of belongingness. We need to be connected in order to feel fulfilled.

Autonomy is the universal urge to be in charge of our own lives—not to be independent of others necessarily, but not to be controlled by them, either. We want to know that we're ultimately in charge. We can make our own decisions. We want to know that we have the freedom to control and determine the outcome of our existence.

What Drs. Deci and Ryan showed, which has been confirmed through years of additional research, is that these psychological needs are universal. They are innate in all human beings. They are instinctual and not learned. They are seen in humanity across time, gender, and culture.

Want proof? Look no further than the gaming industry. The playing of video games has now surpassed the popularity of watching TV. People spend a total of nearly 3 billion hours per week playing video games.[5] Three billion hours! It's estimated that three out of every four homes in America own a video game console. Anecdotally, most kids I ask tell me they would rather play video games than watch a movie or participate in just about any other previously popular form of entertainment. But it's not just kids. The average age of gamers has increased to 35.

Why?

Because video games tap directly into our innate psychological needs.

Research done by Andrew Przybylski, PhD, Scott Rigby, PhD, and Dr. Ryan showed that the reason for the incredible popularity of video games is because they provide outlets for people's innate needs.[6] Completing each new level in a game is an (addictive) exploitation of our need for competence. Playing interactive games that connect us in real time with other players taps into our need for relatedness. And by controlling an avatar and "self-determining" the general situation or outcome of a game, we find a form of autonomy that we often feel we're incapable of achieving in real life.

According to the research, people who play video games aren't trying to escape from themselves. They're actually trying (whether they realize it or not) to get closer to their ideal selves—the people they really want to be.

"The attraction to playing video games and what makes them fun is that it gives people the chance to think about a role they would ideally like to take and then get a chance to play that role," said lead researcher Dr. Przybylski. "I was heartened by the findings which showed that people were not running away from themselves but running towards their ideals. They are not escaping to nowhere, they are escaping to somewhere."[7]

The creators of video games play directly into our deep-rooted psychological needs, and they know it. But it's not just video games that are exploiting our deep desires. The idea of gamification has swept into other fields, too. The U.S. Army uses simulation-style gaming as a recruiting tool at malls across America. Weight-loss and fitness companies use gaming techniques to inspire customers to track their goals and compete for results. Financial websites use gaming-style "play" to demystify money management and investing.

More and more companies and institutions are tapping into the innate psychological desires in the Self-Determination Theory in order to increase their client bases and their profits. How many formerly boring loyalty programs now involve collecting points, achieving levels, sharing on social media, and a level of customization and control that makes people feel a greater connection and loyalty to these brands and services?

Our deep, innate needs are being exploited by the marketplace, even though we don't even realize it. Why? Because the needs articulated by the Self-Determination Theory are real, innate, and important.

Dr. Deci himself said his findings prove that our innate needs are as essential to optimal functioning and well-being "as water, minerals, and sunshine are essential for plants to bloom."[8]

But should we really leave the fulfillment of our innate needs to video game producers and corporate marketing departments? Why let them dictate how our needs are fulfilled when we could learn how to fulfill them ourselves and in more meaningful ways?

GOING DEEPER STILL

It's astounding that we live in an era in which science has identified our innate needs. But if that were enough, then we would all feel satisfied in life. The fact is, we still have questions: Where did these psychological needs come from? Why these needs and not others? And how do we truly fulfill them?

It's time to go deeper. It's time to search for answers that science has yet to deliver. It's time to open our eyes to answers that have been right in front of us—or, more accurately, locked inside of us—forever.

In order to fully understand the genesis of our needs and gain insights into how we can best satisfy them, we have to come at it from a different angle. We have to look outside the box. As we reach the edge of what science has yet to offer, let's expand our lens, take a look back through human history, and dig down to the core of our spiritual knowledge.

Then, and only then, can we unlock the answers to what it takes to properly fulfill our needs.

CHAPTER 6

UNITY: THE SURPRISING CONNECTION BETWEEN SPIRITUALITY AND OLYMPIC HOCKEY

"We are not human beings having a spiritual experience. We are spiritual beings having a human experience."

—PIERRE TEILHARD DE CHARDIN,
20TH-CENTURY FRENCH PHILOSOPHER

One of the most exciting developments in the past few decades is the emergence of research in areas that were once considered "nonscientific." Subjects such as mindfulness, positive psychology, happiness, and innate needs are now studied in academia, where just a few years ago they may have been scoffed at for not being "real" science.

One area that researchers are exploring in the midst of this mindful renaissance is the impact of spirituality on our lives. And because of this pursuit, for the first time in modern history, more and more people are starting to appreciate that in order to achieve true satisfaction in life, we need to grow both our bodies and our souls.

There seems to be plenty of evidence that our metaphysical needs are hungering for nutrients that are missing. The Self-Determination Theory itself is built on the concept that people still feel some level of lack, despite having their material needs met. The missing vibrancy, the lack of intrinsic motivation that isn't being satisfied in the obvious way—by just giving people more stuff—means there is something deeper going on. The fact that you can't just pay somebody a larger bonus or scare somebody into working with enthusiasm shows that we are a lot more complex than we may have believed in the past. Our innate needs are deeper than the material, and if we don't fulfill them properly, we feel—quite rightfully—that we're lacking.

That's why transcendence is such a big business today. People all over the world are searching for transcendence through retreats that take them to some exotic locale to "transcend" the mundaneness of everyday life. Why would people be willing to spend thousands of hard-earned dollars and gobs of precious time in the hopes of finding some measure of transcendence? It's because we have something internal that makes us to yearn to be inspired. And that something is our spirituality.

No matter how often most of us ignore it in our daily existence, there are times we're caught off guard and stand in awe knowing we've touched greatness, when we've done something deeply satisfying. It could be that feeling of accomplishment when you see the fruits of your sacrifice for a cause you believe in; that feeling of joy when you see the child in whom you've invested so much grow up, become independent, and give back; or maybe that feeling of purpose when you see the gratitude on the face of the person who benefited from your care or generosity.

Sometimes, we experience moments that leave us feeling exuberant, uplifted, better than ever. We feel connected to the world around us. We feel that we exist beyond just our bodies, fulfilling a need to be part of the something that's bigger, part of the metaphysical.

These moments can happen when you're driving down the road and come around a corner and witness the most amazing sunset you've ever seen. They can happen when you hold your newborn baby for the first time. They can happen at weddings, when the connectedness of family and friends all swirl together and lift us up in an atmosphere where we once again believe love is possible and the future is bright. For some people, they can happen in a church, mosque, or synagogue or in a meditation stance. They can happen on the playing field. They can happen when we're working on something and we get a flash of inspiration—a thought, a direction, an insight we never had before, which seems to come from someplace outside of ourselves. Songwriters and artists talk about these sorts of "inspirations" all the time, but the home builder, the pilot, and the accountant experience them, too. (Okay, maybe not the accountant.)

When you have one of those transcendent or inspiring moments, you can't help but feel there is something about the experience that is tangibly different than anything else you feel in your day-to-day existence.

That feeling is a taste of the spiritual.

That feeling is our sense that there is something bigger. Something universal. Something divine. It's as if we no longer see many different objects or even the pieces of a puzzle. We see one pulsating life. We are awestruck by its harmony, beauty, and unity.

Why do we feel this way? Where does that feeling come from? How do I know that you've felt it when we've never even met? Are these feelings truly universal?

MY TRIP TO SAFED

Just before I started law school, I traveled to Israel. I wanted to see the birthplace of some of the world's great religions, and I wound up receiving an education that exceeded my every expectation. One day, I sat in on a class on spirituality at an academic center in Jerusalem. As the professor presented his ideas, I kept questioning him at every turn. (I guess I was a little amped up for law school.) At the end of his lecture, he approached me. "I noticed you've got a lot of questions," he said. "I can connect you to a really wise man, one of the world's foremost experts on Kabbalah. He's only about three hours north of here."

"Yes! I would love that," I said.

So on a whim, I hopped on a bus for a three-hour journey to a hilltop in the mystical city of Safed. (I'm still not 100 percent sure if the professor was just getting rid of me so he could teach his class in peace.)

A lot of people have heard of Kabbalah, since it took a turn into pop culture in the early 2000s, embraced by certain pop stars and actors in search of some deeper meaning in their lives. What's confusing to some who've only heard the word bandied about in magazines is that Kabbalah is not a religious denomination. It's a systematic formulation of mystical truths and teachings that, many believe, predates the inception of world religions. It has influenced philosophers, scientists, psychologists, and religious leaders throughout history.[1] So it's kind of a big deal, and meeting one of the foremost Kabbalah experts in the world was a very big deal to me at 21 years old.

Stepping off the bus onto the cobblestone streets of Safed was awe-inspiring. I found myself surrounded by buildings that had been standing since the 1600s and streets filled with pious individuals who spent their days studying ancient wisdom. I wandered those streets in my jeans and baseball cap, searching for the address handed to me on a scrap of paper. Eventually, I found it. I knocked on an old wooden door, and a woman answered. I told her who I was, who sent me, and why I had come. She smiled at me as if I were her own son. She invited me into her tiny apartment, a space that wasn't much bigger than my parents' dining room. She walked me into a tiny study, where a bearded man sat behind a modest desk, surrounded by shelves filled with hundreds of books—wall-to-wall, floor-to-ceiling. In the lamplight of that dimly lit room, I could swear this man's face was glowing.

I told him why I'd come. I had questions about the meaning of life, what I wanted to be, and how best to navigate that journey.

He smiled at me and asked, "What do you want out of life"?

I knew this answer. I could recite the list backward and forward, in my sleep. "I want a meaningful career, family, contribution to society, wealth, wisdom, love, season tickets . . . "

He wasn't even paying attention. I looked back at him after my soliloquy to see his head down, scribbling something on a piece of paper. He moved the paper across the table. I looked down. It had one word written on it: "Unity."

I didn't miss a beat. "Of course I want unity," I quickly responded, realizing I was in front of a man who has clearly eschewed materialism for loftier pursuits. "I pray we see a time when we can all get along, no war, peace . . . "

He smiled at me again. This time it was different. It was the way you smile at your 2-year-old when you realize she has no clue what you're talking about.

"What you really want is unity," he said.

I smiled, confused, and realized that the best thing I could do was to stop talking and listen.

"All of us are striving for the same thing," he began. "You want a certain quality of life experience that you can't even articulate. Your goals are just physical reflections of your desire to get that feeling. What you are really seeking is called transcendence. It's something that feels qualitatively different than what you are accustomed to, which is why you're striving for it."

That definitely got my attention. He turned around and pulled a book off his shelf and began what would stretch into a 3-hour discussion, bolstered by volume after volume of works by spiritual masters. Those works all spoke to the supernatural moments; to the intense raptures and lucidity that exceed normal perceptions; to those moments when we feel something swelling inside us—that metaphysical *something.* The descriptions matched what I intuitively knew but could never articulate. These ancient books and texts described those moments that feel *awesome,* when we feel invincible and when the gap between the life we have and the life we want instantly closes.

We spoke about the fact that for most of us, this feeling only happens in brief moments throughout our lives. Since we have no words to properly describe these moments, and since they seem so impossible to capture, we simply accept a life in which our everyday "reality" just isn't all that inspiring. We wind up watching other people do interesting things as a weak substitute for our own transcendence, and we distract ourselves through nonstop entertainment—spending large portions of our days scrolling through phones and binge-watching Netflix. Or we search for "highs" through drugs or alcohol.

The greatest tragedy in life, the sage explained, is that we don't realize that moments of transcendence, these awesome feelings, are available to us in a sustained form through a process of mental, emotional, and spiritual evolution.

"You mean we can feel that sort of transcendence all the time?" I asked.

He smiled at me again, this time knowingly.

I was hooked. I wanted to know more. That's when he put it into high gear.

"The world draws its sustenance from one Unifying Energy. This Unified Energy has many names throughout history, and It binds every aspect in the universe to us and Itself. We yearn to connect to It because we stem from It. We are a spark from that Unified Energy. Physically, our bodies are separate from each other, but on a deeper level, that of spirituality, we are all interconnected through Unified Energy, the vast spiritual network. Moments of transcendence are manifestations of the times we connect to that Energy. That connection, which flows through our own spiritual sparks, is what feels different."[2]

Little did I know then, but these concepts that were brand new to me weren't new at all. What the sage was talking about had been at the core of discussion, exploration, and investigation from time immemorial.

Ever since humans began trying to understand the reality around them and within them, they have sensed this Unified Energy. They have felt that the multiplicity, the strife, and the division of things are only outer layers; that there exists within everything a *single* life, a world soul (as it were) that when tapped into brings ultimate happiness and exhilaration. The history of human endeavors has been one of trying to make this Unified Energy manifest.

In the earliest philosophies of western civilization, Parmenides declared the "way of truth" to be the realization of the singularity of Being. Plotinus described the deepest yearning of the soul as a return to the state of basking in "the One." Over a millennium later, Spinoza used analytical logic and propositions to attempt to explain the Unity of the All. Leibniz differed by calling Unified Energy "monads," including some different details but overall expounding on the same theme.

In the 1700s, Immanuel Kant proved the human mind incapable of plunging to the depth of the "noumena," meaning the idea that something can exist without being affected by perception. But the German idealist school of Fichte, Hegel, and Schelling still insisted on the existence of an Absolute Spirit synthesizing the harmony of everything. And for two centuries after, thought has continued to revolve around these contentions. Romantic poetry and literature throughout the 19th century seemed like one long constant attempt to emotionally relate to this fundamental truth that the mind cannot seem to logically put into words.

In the 20th and 21st centuries, empirical science has only come to strengthen these observations. The underlying driver of Albert Einstein's scientific experiments was his desire to unify different branches of physics. As Einstein said, "It is a glorious feeling to discover the unity of a set of phenomena that seem to first be completely separate."[3]

The study of physics is man's attempt to understand our universe, or more accurately, to formulate relations between the phenomena of nature. The quest to unify the sometimes conflicting laws of nature has been the elusive goal for the most brilliant physicists of modern times and perhaps of history. Theories such as quantum physics and string theory identify a unified and singular force that dictates all interactions in the universe. Science has shown that everything—from trees to polar bears, from the sun to the grass, from the milk in your fridge to the farthest galaxy in the universe, may appear at the surface to be distinct, but on a deeper level are all parts of the same whole as they are made of the same energy that flows through everything. As theoretical physicist and Nobel-laureate Steven Weinberg once said "We want to achieve a simpler understanding of nature. And the path to simplicity is unification."[4]

And all along the way, throughout the millennia of man's philosophic and scientific development, the impetus for many of the world's religions stemmed from this intuitive recognition of a reality within, and beyond, oneself and the inner yearning to access this reality.[5]

There are many different names for it, religious and nonreligious. But what the sage was pointing me toward was the concept that all of these different names are describing the very same—universal—thing: unity.

"It sounds incredible," I told the sage. "However, I am studying to be a lawyer, not a mystic. How do *I* tap into that energy?"

His answer: "You're already plugged in. You just need to stop blocking the connection."

THE ELECTRICAL CONNECTION

The sage's teachings didn't inspire me so much as they enlightened me. He taught me about concepts I never knew existed, which allowed me to integrate them into my life. Hearing these concepts was, for me, like turning on a light—or, perhaps more accurately, seeing the man in the minivan. Once you gain the context, once it's part of your schema, you can suddenly see it in everything.

And so, as I embarked on my legal career and my business career and my marriage and my coaching my kids' sports teams— all the regular parts of my life—I was now able to use that insight to find spirituality in things that might otherwise seem mundane.

Like a house that has dozens of electric outlets and appliances, the world is filled with physical objects (people, animals, plants, etc.). But in that house, the electricity flows through one source, and while it may be allocated differently, it's unified in that each outlet draws from the same energy. So to in our world. Each of us may be separate, but we draw the energy of our existence from a single unified energy source, that thing the sage called Unified Energy. Everyone around you is alive because of their connections to Unified Energy. That's the core of who they are: each separate, each unique, each with their own contribution, but the same in where they draw their essential life force.

Our body is meant to be nurtured and strengthened, but it's just a receptacle, a vessel for our spiritual spark.

This is why we desire transcendence: It's the pleasure we feel when we connect to Unified Energy. It happens when we feel connected to something more than ourselves—with nature, with people, with a cause. Nothing in the material world can compete, nor could any sensory experience compare, with the depth of metaphysical fulfillment.

So how do we connect to this Unified Energy?

THE SCHEMA OF SELF

As the sage revealed to me, we are already connected to the energy. What that means is that we have all the spirituality we will ever need already loaded in. It's the essence of who we are. The issue is not becoming more connected; it's removing the blocks to the connection we already have. Like a person sitting in a dark room complaining about the lack of sunlight, the answer is not to hope for sunshine, it's to open the shades.

The block to Unified Energy stems from our schemas. Do you remember how the schema can filter things out of our conscious mind? Well, schemas are the gateways to our soul, too. They can either block the light or let it shine through.

One way to see the world around us is through the prism of selfishness. We assess situations based on whether they benefit us. By doing that, we see ourselves as a separate entity from others. As we focus more on ourselves, our desires, our entitlements, our gripes, we create more neuroconnections that fill our schemas with existential separateness. So even if we get what we want, it feels empty since we've blocked our unity with the world around us; we've blocked the access to Unified Energy. That could be why so many of our accomplishments leave us feeling hollow.

On the other hand, the more we limit the self, the more we become absorbed into the greater whole. Selflessness—seeing our self as interconnected to others—enhances our schematic filter in how we see the world. I'm not talking about the loss of self. In fact, our uniqueness is critical. I'm talking about seeing the self as a part of something greater. The less we see ourselves as the center of our lives, the bigger we become and the better we feel. It's counter-rational to see it this way, but the less your life is *about* you, the better it is *for* you. As you limit self, you transcend to something greater and experience deeper pleasure and fulfillment.

Need an example of what this all means? I know I did. And as with so many things in life, we often learn lessons in the least expected ways. Years after visiting the sage in Safed, I found myself watching a sports movie called (of all things) *Miracle* and saw these concepts come to life in perfect clarity on the screen.

THE UNITY OF MIRACLE

One of the greatest moments in United States sports history was the victory of the U.S. Men's hockey team over the USSR in its quest for gold in the 1980 Olympic Games. In 2004, the movie *Miracle* tried to capture it for posterity. Kurt Russell played Coach Herb Brooks, the mastermind coach who turned that team into legend.

For modern-day fans, it's hard to appreciate this, but back in 1980, professional athletes were ineligible to play in the Olympics.

The Olympics were purely a competition for "amateur," or non-professional, athletes.

That year, the greatest hockey team in the world, by far, was the USSR. Since the team was not part of any professional league, it was able to compete in the Olympics—even though the team's members dedicated their lives to hockey and practiced together year-round as one team—and every single player was the caliber of a professional athlete. For the United States and most other teams heading into those Games, it was clearly an unfair fight.

To give it some extra context, this all unfolded at the height of Cold War tensions between the two countries. At every turn, the United States and the Soviet Union were actively fighting to prove their superiority on the planet, be it through sports, space flight, or the development of nuclear weapons and defense systems.

Against all this tension, the U.S. team was made up of college players: young, inexperienced, and divided. Many of them had played against each other in college and were still holding on to those rivalries. These feuds were so strong that during one practice early on in training, a fight broke out between the players.

Coach Brooks realized the internal tensions were too high to continue practice, let alone lead to any sort of victory. He stopped practice and had the players gather in a circle. One by one, he had them go around, each stating their names, hometowns, and the teams they played for. He hoped that they would start to see each other as human beings all on the same team, rather than still back home fighting for college glory. But they didn't. He decided he would have them do this regularly. Each and every day, they would state their names, their hometowns, and the teams they played for—and their responses were always the same.

In the players' minds, their loyalties remained with their universities, and as they stated their name and hometown, the answer to the question "Who do you play for?" was always their respective college.

The team's exhibition game against Norway was disastrous, and Brooks finally had enough. So after the game, he blocked the entrance to the locker room and told the team to line up on the goal line to skate "drills." Back and forth and back and forth they went, and each time the athletes thought a drill was over, Brooks screamed, "Again!" He pushed them to the point of exhaustion—the assistant coach begged him to stop, and the staff in the arena turned off the lights.

Showing no mercy as they skated back and forth in darkness, Brooks finally screamed at them, "When you put on that jersey, you represent yourself and your teammates, and the name on the front is more important than the one on the back!"

The players could barely move. Brooks didn't care. He made them keep on skating.

Finally, one player got it. He screamed out, "Mike Eruzione, Winthrop, Massachusetts."

Brooks, realizing that Eruizone was trying to make a point in answering the first two questions even without being asked, turned to him and asked, "Who do you play for?"

Eruzione heaved with exhaustion and said, "I play . . . for the United States of America!"

Brooks paused for a moment and said, "That's all, gentlemen." He walked off the ice as the players collapsed in relief.

That powerful scene highlighted a deeper spiritual principle, the one the sage scribbled on the paper in Safed: the indispensable value of unity and the process by which one achieves it.

The 1980 U.S. Hockey Team wasn't talented enough to win as a collection of individuals. In order to succeed, they needed to become one cohesive unit. One team. Together, and only together, could the organism (as well as the individuals) achieve greatness.

Brooks, in an extreme way, was trying to shift their schemas— to have his college athletes see themselves not as individuals, but as parts of the same team, a team that represented something far greater than any college: It represented a country. "The name on the front (USA) is more important than the one on the back (their individual names)" was Brooks' way of asking them to not nullify their selves, but nullify their selfishness.

As the movie progressed, that nullification of self-focus and self-absorption changed the way the players felt about each other and themselves, the level of sacrifice they were willing to endure, and the resounding success that they ultimately achieved. It all emerged from that one concept of unity—of connecting to unified energy of the cause: representing one's country.

As the famed theologian Thomas Merton put it, "We are already one. But we imagine that we are not. And what we have to recover is our original unity. What we have to be is what we are."[6]

THE DEFAULT SETTING

That's how life works. We think being selfish is acting in our best interest, but it's actually preventing us from becoming the best we can be. It taints how we feel about ourselves, how we feel about the people around us, and how much we will sacrifice for what we believe in.

We are like this because that's how we started. Children begin their lives focused on their needs to the exclusion of others. A baby exhibits constant self-centeredness. They *always* need *everything, immediately*. A newborn wakes up at 3 a.m. hungry. She will never say to herself, "You know, Mom's been at this for days on end. I mean, look at her. I don't think she's showered since Sunday. I ate 2 hours ago and will eat again in a few hours. I know I'm a little hungry, but maybe I ought to let her sleep until dawn."

Nope. It's "waaahhhhhh!" every single time.

But at some point, we are supposed to evolve beyond that. Let's face it, we all know a few so-called adults who have the same mentality as when they were 2 months old. They behave as though the world should revolve around them, as if their purpose in life is to take from everyone, all the time, just to satisfy their own desires.

We may even understand their motivation: Selfishness allows for momentary pleasure. It's instant, so it feels good for a moment. We all crave immediate gratification. I think most of us, however, recognize that the hit of feeling good disappears quickly. So we crave something deeper. How do we satisfy that craving? There is only one way. We need to allow ourselves to spiritually mature. To evolve. To convert our selfishness to become more and more selfless. Because learning to be selfless in everything we do is how we remove the blocks to existential fulfillment.

Every moment we choose either to connect to Unified Energy or to block it. And it is in that choice that we can tap into the essence of reality; the ultimate source of all growth, of life, of inner strength, and ability.

How do we apply this our everyday lives? First, we need a better understanding of the forces within our souls.

CHAPTER 7

TROPHIES, SYMBOLS, AND THE FORCES WITHIN

"Try not to become a man of success. Rather become a man of value."

—ALBERT EINSTEIN

Why was my friend Dave (from the Introduction) not jumping for joy about his life? Based on almost any standard, he was doing well. His life was not in any imminent danger; he had plenty of food to eat and nice shelter; he had love (even if his relationship was a bit strained); he had access to and time for entertainment and relaxation (even if it wasn't as much as he wanted); and statistically speaking, he made more money than the vast majority of people on earth. So what's the problem?

The same could be said for so many people. Why are many

college students so stressed that they're barely able to function?[1] Why are more people in their fifties and sixties getting divorced, quitting their jobs, and trying to "find" themselves? Did you know that today, depression is the leading cause of disability in the United States for ages 15 to 44.[2] The average age for the onset of depression is now 14 years old.[3] Fourteen years old!

What about you? Are you happy with life? Do you feel like you should be more or have more? Why isn't mere survival enough for us in this chaotic and dangerous world? Why do we feel like something is missing?

The answer I shared with Dave is the same for most people: It's because we are ignoring our deep-rooted spiritual needs.

We can have all the material pleasures that modern society has to offer, and we can even satisfy our innate psychological needs. But if we ignore our spiritual needs, we will not be fully satisfied with life.

In Dave's case, he was missing out on the spiritual fulfillment of his psychological need for competence and mastery. Sure, he had tons of competence. He had mastered a lot! But the job, the house, the car, the entertainment system, even his marriage and kids— none of those made Dave happy because of the relationship he had *to* them. They were his accomplishments. They served his life's pursuits.

It didn't occur to him to serve *them*.

What Dave needed to do was change his perspective. The Self-Determination Theory gives us an insight as to our innate needs, but unless we satisfy those needs through a schema of selflessness, we will still feel empty. We may be intrinsically motivated, but we will still feel an existential lacking. Dave was doing just that. He was fulfilling his need for mastery but in a selfish manner. As such, he was blocking his connection to Unified Energy. In fact, in the pursuit of fulfilling his innate needs, he was separating himself from others. He may have been "winning," but it didn't matter because he wasn't being fulfilled.

"We both grew up in a world that taught us the winner in life is the one with the most trophies. Awards, status, titles are all symbols of success, and you've been very good at collecting symbols," I said to him. "But you feel empty because you *are* empty. You have a need for mastery and that's innate, but you're not satisfying that need properly. A symbol will only feel good while you're in the process of getting it. But once you have it, once it's on your shelf, once you get into that school or get that promotion or see your bonus check or win that game, you don't feel satisfied for long. It goes away, and you feel empty again."

"I don't get it," Dave interjected. "Are you saying I shouldn't be ambitious? I shouldn't work hard to achieve big goals?"

"No," I said. "You live with a ton of desire. That's great. Call it grit, hustle, ambition, whatever. It shows you're alive. But your desire so far has been selfish in nature. Everything you're doing is trying to satisfy yourself, and so everything feels empty. Your marriage is about how your wife meets your needs, and she's not doing that so you're disappointed. Your job is about how much money you make, so you're lacking real connection to your colleagues and clients. Your relationship to your children is based on whether they're becoming the people *you* want them to be, rather than giving them the support to become who *they* should be. When you put conditions on your love, you're taking. You have moments when you feel good, but the relationship is built on a shaky foundation. And as your kids grow up, you grow apart."

He looked a little dejected.

"Look, I'm not faulting you for any of this. We *all* do this. We're born this way. When you give a child a cookie, he opens his hand for another. When a toddler sees a toy, he takes it. That's how we start life. But spiritual growth is up to us. It's our free will, and if we don't actively pursue it, then it's never going to happen. The goal of life should be to transform that initial desire to *take* into the spiritual desire to *serve*. That's where we connect to Unified Energy."

There was something in that part of the conversation that lit a spark within him. I could see it in his eyes. I think it was when I stated the "goal of life." Dave was good at setting goals and accomplishing them. I was now speaking his language.

"You can start with small goals and see where it goes," I said. "The key is to think past yourself—that's the point of spiritual connection and that's when moments feel different. When you support your children and let them shine, you swell with an inner feeling of pride. When you are standing in front of a picturesque scene in nature, you feel small—and that, ironically enough, makes you feel bigger."

"Yeah, I guess," he said.

"When you hold a door for someone and share a smile, you feel better, like things are okay in the world. Why? Because that's how it works. As you limit self, you transcend to something greater and experience deeper pleasure and fulfillment."

"So, what, you want me to hold doors for people?" Dave said. "That sounds a little simplistic, you know. I've got so many problems, and—"

"That's exactly what I'm saying. In fact, the next time you're upset, try something for me," I said. "No matter what it is, the next time you're upset about something, go and perform a random act of kindness."

"Oh, come on. That's so—"

"Ridiculous? I know. It sounds ridiculous. But try it. When you're upset, do a small act of kindness for someone else. Hold the door open for a stranger, smile at the cashier, or randomly compliment your colleague. Anything. See if you can remain upset *during* the act. You'll find that you can't. Once you're giving, you're connected to a deeper energy and you can't feel that negativity. When you realize how powerful that is in those little moments, try it in the bigger moments. Try it with your wife. With your kids. At work. Just try."

Dave sort of nodded and shook his head at the same time.

"Okay," he said. He seemed somewhat disappointed by how simple it sounded. People are so impressed by complexity, and this sounded too unsophisticated to work. Still, he added, "I'll try it."

And off he went, disappearing back into the throngs of pedestrians on the sidewalks of New York City.

LESSONS OF THE TWIN TOWERS

As I watched Dave walk away, I couldn't help but think back to 9/11. I was in the subway when the planes struck the Twin Towers. After my train was redirected and I wound up above ground again, I was still in Manhattan, just a few miles away from the towers. When they fell, I felt the earth shake beneath my feet. I watched the smoke billow into the air, knowing in that moment that had I taken a different subway line or lined up a different set of appointments that day, my life could have been directly affected or even ended, then and there.

Millions of other New Yorkers experienced the same thing, while hundreds of millions more outside of the city experienced something close while watching those horrific events unfold on their televisions.

There's something that happens when you grapple with mortality: It puts life into perspective. And in some cases, it changes us.

In this case, what I witnessed in the aftermath of that tragedy was something glorious. People prayed for each other. They volunteered for each other. They came home from work and watched hours of news coverage just to see if strangers were reconnected with their loved ones. Firefighters drove in from around the country, through the night, just to help; and then thousands of New Yorkers walked to Ground Zero to offer food, drinks, and even back massages to the rescue workers as they continued the impossible labor of searching for any signs of life in the rubble. The media would go on and on about the resiliency of New Yorkers, how we had the will and the fight to recover and rebuild. But what many New Yorkers will tell you is that they witnessed something more, even if they don't have the words to describe it.

As the cleanup stretched on into October, and the immediacy of the horror started to wear off, the connectedness continued in New York. In the hyper-fast pace of midtown Manhattan, people stopped and held doors for each other. Men in business suits helped mothers carry baby strollers down the subway steps at Union Square. People looked each other in the eye and smiled as they crossed the streets near Rockefeller Center. I noticed more people than ever sharing conversations with their cab drivers or the men and women behind the counters at the bodegas.

That tremendous sense of connectedness flourished everywhere you went in the weeks after 9/11. Then, as time went on, we forgot our mortality, our vulnerability, and life went back to "normal."

When life is safe and secure, we have a tendency to focus on ourselves. But during those periods when we realize that our time here is limited, that the world as we know it is fragile, we start to see through the eyes of our soul, which always directs us to become more selfless. It is in these moments when our schemas see past race and religion, past our idiosyncratic surfaces, to something deeper.[4]

It is in that depth where we find our greatness.

THE TWO PURSUITS

There aren't many of us who can dedicate our lives to the study of spirituality. Most of us can't imagine hunkering down in a little room in Safed searching for answers in ancient texts, the same way we can't imagine becoming a brain surgeon or a rocket scientist. But we don't have to become any of those things in order to learn from them and benefit from their findings.

When we look to the Bible or to some of the greatest philosophers and theologians throughout history, we realize that Dr. Edward Deci and Dr. Richard Ryan didn't discover new innate needs; they were simply turning the scientific method toward unlocking the truth behind ideas that we've been talking about for centuries.

In particular, two needs described in the Self-Determination Theory are scientific descriptions for a well-established spiritual concept: that there are two driving forces at work in every human being. These forces are two equally powerful energies that our soul contains and that manifest into two lifelong pursuits: the pursuit of significance and the pursuit of connectedness.

IN THE BEGINNING

In 1965, Rabbi Joseph Soloveitchik, PhD, one of the most impactful theologians of the 20th century—a man who taught thousands of students during his lifetime—wrote an essay entitled "Lonely Man of Faith."[5] That essay was like a theological explosion and has since spurred thousands of hours of discussion, analysis, and commentary by academics, theologians, and bestselling authors.[6] Soloveitchik's insights have provided clarity in how we understand the core elements of our soul.

In the essay, Dr. Soloveitchik dug into a deep exploration of the first 10 verses of Genesis and the two different creation stories of

Adam and Eve in order to elicit a dual paradigm. He explored the first account, in which mankind was given a mandate to be fruitful and multiply, to subdue the earth, and have dominion over nature. He parsed out the Biblical words to show how we are driven to accomplish and be successful, and were imbued with a divine ability to achieve dominance and mastery over the environment. This significance-driven side of ourselves measures success by achievements.

But then, through the second account, he described a very different side of our human souls. Formed from the dust of the earth, mankind is portrayed as passive and introspective. As opposed to having mastery over the environment, we yearn for our place within it. It is in this spiritual energy that we yearn for another—a relationship born not from convenience or partnership, but from mutual sacrifice. This side of us is charged not with world domination, but instead with something simpler, yet deeper: connection. It's a human quest for personal meaning and mutually fulfilling relationships among people, the environment, and the Divine.

The Soloveitchik paradigm speaks directly to two of our scientifically proven psychological needs: those of mastery and of relatedness—the need to conquer and accomplish, and the need to relate and be understood by others.

This paradigm is the delicate balance between one's focus on self and one's focus on others. The bridge between the "self" (our quest for personal significance) and the "other" (our desire to connect to those around us) are two fundamental aspects of our humanity that need to be explored, understood, and satisfied.

Philosophers have wrestled with this for centuries. Much of Erik Erikson's psychological developmental theories are about trying to strike this proper balance. In fact, one can summarize much of 20th-century existential philosophy—from Heidegger to Sartre, and Buber to Levinas—as the attempt to reconcile Being-in-Self with Being-for-Other.[7]

Political philosophies throughout history—from Machiavelli to Hobbes, and Plato's *Republic* to Marx's communist manifesto—have been about trying to work out one's rights and obligations, one's autonomy and subjugation to the community, and one's responsibility to a neighbor and one's need to maintain individuality.[8]

Hillel, a first-century scholar, succinctly describes this struggle in his famous question: "If I am not for myself, who will be for me? But if I am only for myself, what am I?"[9]

Self and other. Significance and connectedness. This duality makes up the entirety of our spiritual needs and the forces behind all of our desires.

The need for significance is the energy that gives us the capacity and ambition to accomplish great things; to rise past it all and achieve. It's the part of us that responds to tasks and goals, the part that needs to win. It's the desire to grow, to make a difference in this world and leave our mark on it. Significance is not a want, it's a need—and if we neglect it, we will feel existentially unsuccessful.

The energy of connectedness is that of caregiver, the one that finds its worth through its relationship to others. This aspect of our soul understands that the greatest thing we can achieve is a connection to another person.

In speaking of these two identities, Soloveitchik notes that "neither one exists in a vacuum, and that the ideal [hu]man oscillates between the two as required."[10]

So, how do we satisfy these two seemingly opposing aspects of our souls and access the transcendence that brings exhilaration to life?

For now, let's focus on the energy of significance, which is what Dave struggled with. (We'll get deeper into connectedness in the next chapter.)

THE COUNTERFEIT SIGNIFICANCE

Why is it that Dave—and the rest of us—wind up pursuing goals that don't fulfill our true need for significance?

It's because we mistake what we want for what we need.

If you recall from the Chapter 5, we pursue our desires (our wants) because we think they will satisfy our needs. Although there are myriad ways to satisfy each need, we pick a path not because it's the best method or the most efficient; we pick the path that we know, that we have experienced and expect to satisfy us. Many times the paths we pick, the desires we have, aren't our own. They've been generated by the society around us.

The need for significance is innate. We are born with it. It's in our soul. We've been driven by it from the start. Ever since we were little, we've been vying to feel important. We felt that need (even though we couldn't identify it), and then we immediately started to get feedback from the outside world as to how to fulfill it.

As we navigated through life, we entered into established mini-societal structures such as families, schools, or close-knit communities, and were given the rules of significance for those mini-societies. The items that a particular mini-society deemed significant became our own pursuits, and the reactions of those around us reinforced our neurological programming, which only created stronger neurological connections and a more focused schema that instructed us to do more of the same.

How did we measure our significance? Well, every society has its symbols of significance: grades, trophies, clothes, and phones were just the beginning. As we got older, we continued to collect symbols to prove our worth: houses, cars, titles, romantic partners, and more.

But collecting symbols isn't enough to feel significant. That's just the beginning. Once you have those symbols, then you need to compare what you have with your peer group to determine how significant you really are. Our pursuit of significance is not about fitting in; it's about standing out. It's about winning, achieving mastery and dominance over your environment. Your test scores don't carry meaning unless you did better than someone else. The university that accepted you feels good when you see its rank compared to your friends' college acceptances. You feel popular on social media only once you find out how many "friends" your classmates have.

The need to collect symbols and then compare them against the symbols of others is a never-ending struggle. As the competition escalates, we yearn to possess symbols of significance even if they cost us things we hold dear. That's why so many people steal, cheat, and harm themselves with drugs to win at that competition, be it academic, athletic, or professional.

Why? Because we are attempting to satisfy our inner need of significance by using some socially agreed-upon metric. We see significance as a measure of how we are seen in the eyes of others. *They* make us feel significant. We need *their* validation for us to feel successful.

So we take jobs, pursue hobbies, and even enter into relationships to increase our societal standing. And as others heap praise, accolades, honor, and respect upon us, we feel as if we've consumed another quick-and-easy microwave dinner: We're full but not nourished.

In Chapter 5, we discussed the Trap of Materialism and how we mistakenly opt for cheaper ways to fulfill our metaphysical needs. We incline to material pleasures because they: (1) are easier to appreciate since we can sense them, (2) are enjoyable only when experienced, and (3) need to be constantly upgraded.

The Trap of Materialism is one of the primary causes of

sadness and confusion for people who have achieved "success." The sensory nature of symbols of success makes it a clear sign of achievement. As we achieve these symbols, we experience moments of enjoyment but not deep-rooted satisfaction. We intuit that we should feel more significant but don't. Since the material pursuits are not based on depth, we are left wanting more. So we look around at those who have more and assume that our dissatisfaction is only because we need to upgrade our symbols. So we dig in and work harder. But until we change what we're working toward, that feeling of true success and fulfillment will elude us.

This never-ending cycle saps true significance and self-worth from us and brings instead self-consciousness. But since this pursuit is an attempt to fulfill a core need, we can't ignore it and, over time, become neurologically conditioned to this misdirection.

So how do we break out of it? How do we feel truly significant and not be trapped into the counterfeit significance?

FINDING TRUE SIGNIFICANCE

King Solomon, who is billed as one of the wisest men to ever walk the earth, is quoted in Ecclesiastes as saying, "It is better to go to a house of mourning than a house of feasting."[11]

Really? From one of the wisest men ever? Who would rather go to a funeral than a party?

King Solomon was getting at a profound concept: Personal growth—and resulting greatness—come from grappling with your mortality.

We are all going to die. All of us. And if more of us grappled with, learned from, and paid attention to that fact, perhaps we would live life more fully. As Ian Fleming, famed author and creator of the James Bond series, said, "You only live twice: Once when you are born and once when you look death in the face."[12]

I'll never forget reading the perspective of psychiatrist Irvin Yalom, MD, regarding his terminally ill cancer patients: "An open confrontation with death allows many patients to move into a mode of existence that is richer than the one they experienced prior to their illness. Many patients report dramatic shifts in life perspective. They are able to trivialize the trivial, to assume a sense of control, to stop doing things they do not wish to do, to communicate more openly with families and close friends, and to live entirely in the present rather than the future or past. . . . Over and over we hear our patients say, 'Why did we have to wait until now, till we are riddled with cancer, to learn how to value and appreciate life?'"[13]

In his reflections on Dr. Yalom's words, Professor Tal Ben-Shahar, PhD, recounts what struck him most about the experiences of cancer patients: "[F]ollowing the news of their terminal disease, they were still the same people, with the same knowledge of life's questions and answers, the same cognitive and emotional capacities. . . . (Yet,) their lives changed. They gained no new knowledge, but, rather, an acute awareness of what they knew all along. In other words, they had within them (all along) the knowledge of how they should live life. It was that they had ignored this knowledge or were not conscious of it."[14]

You have the knowledge of how you should live life. It's already within you. You've had it all along.

WRITING YOUR EULOGY

Let's do a little exercise. I know it may intially feel dark, but bear with me.

Picture your funeral.

You lived a long life, but now it is your day of death. Someone familiar to you mounts the podium to deliver your eulogy. That person looks down at the paper and begins to speak.

What does that person say?

More importantly, what do you *want* them to say?

Take a piece of paper and jot down the top talking points for your own eulogy. (Feel free to use the chart on this page.) Sound simple? It's not. Sound crazy? What's crazy is trying to live life without having clarity about what you want—and need—to accomplish while you're here.

EULOGY

We are all saddened by the passing of my beloved _____ [Fill in depending on who you see giving your eulogy]. He/She lived a full and vibrant life, but yet his/her passing is no less painful. I would like to share what I believed my _____ exemplified most in life. He/She was:
1.
2.
3.
4.
5.

For a downloadable copy of this chart, go to charlieharary.com/book.

If you really think about it, and concentrate on it, this exercise will provide a window through your wants to your needs. You will start to grasp ways that you can uniquely serve. You have the wisdom you need to be truly significant, according to the spiritual meaning of that word, and if, for a brief moment, we can remove the schema of materialism, it will expose what you already know to be important. When you can marry your desires to your spiritual needs, you've hit it. The key is to make sure you dig deep enough until you feel inspired.

Don't allow yourself to be bound by any limitations. Just write and rewrite until you feel like you have a greater understanding of yourself and how you want to be remembered.

Writing a eulogy now enables us to live our lives for the principles we stand for, instead of merely waking up at the concluding stages of life to face the fact that we spent our days driving toward significance but never reached our destination because we were going the wrong way.

DAVE'S RESOLUTION

Months after I sent Dave out into the world with the mission of becoming a giver rather than a taker, he called me up, excited to meet again. This time when we met, he walked in with the same forcefulness as if he were walking into a board meeting aiming to hit a presentation out of the park. He was pumped.

Apparently, the exercises I gave him worked.

"I was ticked off at my boss one day, and I went storming out of my building and to the subway. As I hit the steps, I saw a woman behind me struggling with a big baby stroller overflowing with all of this stuff," he said. "I looked at her, took a breath, and held the stroller for her—and Charlie, that woman smiled and thanked me, and I realized that for a couple of seconds, I had completely let go of my anger. It wasn't there. It was *gone*! So I started doing it more and more. And I started to feel better. Like, a lot better. Every day.

"And then, get this. I thought about what you said about just trying to make my wife's life great—you know, doing things for her instead of 'taking' all the time. And I thought about when we were dating and we took a trip to Paris, and she fell in love with these eclairs at a little shop we stumbled into one morning. It had been a long time, but I Googled it. I couldn't remember the name, but I remembered where it was, so I went on street view, and I found the shop! It was there, and they had a website and everything, and they had shipping options for their pastries. So I spent a fortune to have a box of eclairs shipped over, and it wasn't our anniversary, just a random Wednesday. I brought these eclairs home, and I swear to you, it's like she fell in love with me all over again right then and there. She couldn't believe I remembered the place and that I went to the trouble to track it down for no reason other than she loved them. I don't even like eclairs, so it had nothing to do with me, you know? It was all for her. And man, was she blown away! She woke up the next morning and gave me a kiss as I was rushing out the door. She hadn't done that in, like, forever."

I just sat there smiling, and nodding. "Yeah," I said. "That's love! Love is about giving!"

Dave had grown up thinking that value was found in what he accomplished. Life was a race. If you don't keep adding and upgrading symbols of significance, it was a sign of mediocrity. He had lived with tunnel vision focused on accomplishments, and in that process he would step over other people to get ahead. He grew up in a world based on comparisons, thinking that your success is measured in relation to everyone around you and not based on your personal growth.

People with a strong need for significance compete every day, not with themselves but with their peers. When they win, they usually leave a trail of carcasses behind them. At the moment of victory, they feel good, but over time there is a sense that something is terribly wrong—because it is.

Selfish significance doesn't lead to real relationships, but to relationships of convenience and utility. The people around someone who is self-focused are only there to serve some purpose. Their marriages are about how well their spouses take care of them. They view their familial relationships in context of whether they're helping or hurting their career. Dave was like that. And in order to reach true significance, he needed to shift his perception of significance from what he could *get* to how he could *serve*.

The real impetus for Dave's sudden change was the eulogy exercise. He did it. He sat down. He wrote it out. He took it seriously. He thought about how he wanted to be remembered—and those thoughts mattered. (He went through other exercises, too, which we'll explore in Part III.)

When we realize we are going to end up in the ground, the comparisons to others—the drive for acceptance and "beating people"—start to wane.

We want to be remembered for what we *gave* to the world, not for what we *took*.

That's what is truly significant: accomplishments that change the world (or at least our little part of the world) for the better. Accomplishments that show our generosity, our concern, our care for people, be they strangers or loved ones or somewhere in between. Accomplishments that are all about what we give.

Once Dave had his eulogy in place, he finally gained some clarity on what he really wanted for his life. He identified the intersection of his talents and skills and discovered how best to use these strengths to help people, which is exactly what he went on to do.

At work, Dave shifted himself away from thinking "What can I take from the company?" to an attitude of "What can I give to the company." His boss noticed the additional attention he gave his assignments and the extra effort he put in executing them. Dave got better at his job and enjoyed it more.

As he stopped counting his chips and evaluating every interaction with "What have they done for me?" he started to give more and care more, and he found that he was free to become himself. He didn't give away all his possessions. He still strove for professional success, but he stopped clamoring to get to the top of the hill at somebody else's pace. He started to live by his own desires, those set by a spiritually evolved Dave. His ambitions were now less about what he could get and more about discovering what he had to give.

I'm no marriage counselor, but Dave worked on his marriage, too, simply from the viewpoint of giving. When he gave his wife those eclairs, it started them down a new path—and not a path of endless gift giving. It became about Dave finding ways to give himself to her. His time. His effort. His attention. His moments at dinner without staring at his phone. His decision to turn down a work trip so he could accompany her to her parents' anniversary dinner. His decision to go to bed at the same hour rather than stay up to watch the late shows. All of it led to their marriage growing stronger and Dave growing happier.

He started to experience a new, deeper level of significance—one he'd never experienced in his life. Not significance that depended on the approval of anyone else, but the true significance of fulfilling his soul's desire. By realizing his own need for significance, getting down to what mattered, and digging in to what he really wanted—a satisfaction of his deepest spiritual needs—Dave completely changed his life in a matter of months.

Of course, you may have noticed that by working on finding true significance, Dave crossed over into finding true connectedness as well—not only with his wife, but also at his place of work and in society. It was inevitable. As Soloveitchik would say, neither of our deep spiritual energies exists in a vacuum. It's through the unity of *both* sides of our deepest spiritual selves that we finally make ourselves whole.

CHAPTER 8

THE PASSION OF A 3-YEAR-OLD: HOW TO ENJOY PITCHING A PERFECT GAME

"When you get to my age, you'll really measure your success in life by how many of the people you want to have love you actually do love you."

—WARREN BUFFET

Back when my wife and I were first married, we went to see a movie called *For the Love of the Game*, starring Kevin Costner and Kelly Preston (released in 1999). It was a romantic comedy, which appealed to her, and a sports movie, which appealed to me, so it felt like a perfect match. I rarely hear anyone mention this movie, which means (I'm guessing) that not too many people remember it, so let me explain the basic premise. Billy Chapel, a major league pitcher, played by Costner, is pitching the final game of his life. The movie flashes back and forth between his game and his personal life, in particular the relationship with a woman he's been dating, Preston's character Jane Aubrey.

As Billy continues to retire more and more batters, the film suggests that this old pitcher is about to embark on the greatest accomplishment any pitcher could ever achieve: a perfect game. If you're not a baseball fan, you have to understand the magnitude of that to appreciate what it means. It means pitching nine whole innings without a single batter getting on base. Only a few dozen pitchers throughout history have accomplished this feat. It's rare, unbelievable, and simply perfect.

National television picks up on Billy's final game, and the whole stadium cheers and roars with each pitch. As the game progresses, so does the story of Billy and his love life, but as the game gets more exciting, we learn that his relationship is disintegrating.

Finally, we get to the last inning. First batter: ground out. Second batter: strike out. The crowd is on its feet. Last batter: one strike, two strikes; next pitch, long ball hit deep . . . foul. Billy wipes the sweat off his face. Next pitch: pop up ... and it's caught! Perfect game! The crowd goes crazy, and the cameras flash as his teammates hoist him into the air.

I honestly thought that's where the credits would roll and the movie would end. But instead, after that tremendous high, the next scene showed Billy back in his hotel room after partying the night away. He sits down on the side of his bed, shoulders slumped, and his head down. On the day that should be the greatest of his life, something is clearly missing.

Jane, the love of his life, is about to move to London, and even on this pinnacle day, the thing he's thinking about the most is her.

Since this was billed as a romantic comedy, I don't think it's a spoiler to tell you what comes next. (Plus, you can't "spoil" a film from 1999, can you?) The movie ends with Billy making a mad dash to the airport, where he stops Jane just before she boards the plane, and they reconnect and presumably live happily ever after.

That's when the credits rolled.

I've often thought about that film. For a while, I wasn't sure why. But I think the reason it has such staying power for me is that it cuts right to the heart of one of our deepest human needs. Billy Chapel had achieved everything he thought he wanted in life, but at the moment of success, at the top of the mountain, at the point where he should be awash in the unadulterated pleasure of significance, he realizes: What's the point of achieving success if there is no one share it with?

The second core spiritual need is connectedness. It's the part of us that lives for "other." It's the part that understands we cannot fully connect to our inner spark, nor can we be absorbed in Unified Energy, if we are alone. This is true even if we spend our lives pursuing activities that make us truly significant. Even if we become a true servant to humanity, there is an aspect of our soul that will only feel satisfied through our relationships—relationships that are not the means to a greater end, but that are the ends unto themselves. Through these authentic relationships we gain access to a part of our soul that significance alone simply cannot unlock.

We feel this need most during atypical moments in life, when there's a break in the humdrum of our everyday routines. That's when we realize just how much we need to connect to other people. During life cycle events or holidays. In moments of exhilarating success or debilitating despair. In those moments, we look around, and if there's no one to share it with, it feels like something fundamental is missing. That's because it is. What's missing is the human connection. It's living with others. It's *being* with others. When we have authentic relationships, the good times feel better and the bad times don't feel as bad.

One of the most powerful stories I've ever heard about the need for human connection was relayed to me by my friend Dan Butler. The story was about his father, who was a member of the United States Armed Forces that liberated the concentration camps at the end of World War II. His father liberated one of the camps that imprisoned children. Butler walked in to see hundreds of emaciated kids, most of whom had lost everything and everyone they loved in the world: parents, siblings, grandparents, aunts, uncles, teachers, classmates . . . all were gone. They were dealing with all of this tremendous loss while faced with their own mortality behind walls of barbed-wire fence, starving to death, demoralized, and worked to the bone.

As soon as the soldiers arrived, they decided their first task was to get these kids fed. So they formed two lines and started ladling out soup. Before they could feed all of the children, Butler's line ran out of soup. Butler scraped the ladle at the bottom of the tureen, realizing he had nothing left to give a boy standing in front of him. He felt terrible, so he did the only thing he could think of: He bent down and gave the boy a hug. The entire camp fell silent as all of the other children stopped and stared. Butler stood and looked at the next child in line. He motioned his hands for the child to come forward, and he hugged that child. He could feel the child shudder, too dehydrated even to cry. And as tears welled up in Butler's eyes, the soldier next to him stepped forward and hugged the next child in line. Seeing what was happening, the children in the other soup line (which still had soup) left their hopes of food behind and quickly lined up in what they perceived as the "hug line" instead.

For children who had gone untouched and unloved for so long, the desire for human connection was more powerful than the need to satisfy their own starvation.

Finding connection is essential. In fact, having a deep connection to another human being, especially a long-lasting connection, can be one of the most fulfilling experiences in life.

THE NEED TO CONNECT

This fundamental need to connect is so powerful that people have been known to die when it is lost. The need for genuine relationships is so strong that we can't survive without it. We hear of people dying of a broken heart, and we recognize that it's something that actually happens. In fact, there's a scientific term for broken-heart syndrome: takotsubo cardiomyopathy.[1] It refers to the physical phenomenon of a sudden temporary weakening of the muscular portion of the heart triggered by emotional stress, caused by such disconnections as the death of a loved one or a breakup. A study back in 1969 entitled "Broken Heart: A Statistical Study of Increased Mortality among Widowers" showed that men had a 40 percent increase in mortality during the 6 months after their wives died.[2] Forty percent!

But it's not just death that hurts us, it's the loss of human connection. Research shows that when people lack social connections or feel lonely, they have a higher risk of stroke and heart disease.[3] Julianne Holt-Lunstad, PhD, conducted research showing that feeling alone increases the risk of many diseases by about 30 percent.[4]

Other studies have shown that loneliness causes cellular changes that can make us more susceptible to viral infections and doubles the risk for developing Alzheimer's.[5]

Science seems to confirm what we have known for centuries: We need a connection to others to not only thrive but survive.

RAQUEL'S LOSS OF CONNECTION

Raquel had a connection in life: her husband. She satisfied her need for connectedness through giving to her husband, supporting him and the family they created with everything she had. She built her world around this, and the neuroconnections were built almost entirely around her dedication to her family.

Her schema for giving to her husband was so strong that she didn't even let up in the final years of their marriage, when it seemed clear to people around her that her husband had stopped giving to her. It was no longer a reciprocal relationship. Yet still, she kept all of the energy she could muster flowing in one direction: toward him and her family.

In my ongoing conversation with Raquel, it was clear to me that by the time her husband left, somewhere deep down she actually knew that he wasn't right for her anymore. She just couldn't admit it to herself. She couldn't change her thinking (her schema simply refused to accommodate the new reality) and instead kept hoping that everything would work out.

After he left, she suddenly had nobody to give her energy to, nobody to share herself with. And so, feeling that one form of connection in life had been lost, she started to seek something very different in order to fill the holes she felt in her soul. She began to seek attention. She wanted people to feel bad for her. She wanted her kids to never forget that their dad hurt her. She switched from being driven to *give* to wanting to *take* from the sympathy of others. Of course, people can't handle being around takers for very long. It's exhausting. Raquel became so focused on the negative aspects of her life that it seemed to suck the energy out of everyone around her. That's what was happening to Raquel's children. They started to resist her. They started to pull away. And the more they did, the worse she felt and the more attention she sought, in a seemingly never-ending cycle of "woe is me."

"So you want to change?" I asked. "You want to feel better? You want to improve the relationship with your kids and your family?"

"Yes."

"Then here is my advice: Go out and become a mentor to other divorcees."

"What? I just got divorced? I'm not equipped to—"

"Just be an ear to help," I said. "Take your pain and use it to help others."

Studies show that when people use their pain to help others, it becomes easier for them to go through the pain themselves.[6] I thought it might help for Raquel to think that her pain wasn't purposeless, but instead gave her a certain credibility. She could "be there" for other women.

What I really hoped was that Raquel would be able to use her mentorship as a method to give again. By lending a shoulder and an ear to other women in pain, it might help her start to be a giver again, rather than a taker, which would better satisfy her spiritual need for connection, even if the recipients of her mentorship were total strangers.

All that Raquel was able to see was that her husband was gone, and without him she lost her happiness. What she couldn't see yet was that it wasn't this particular man she needed. Her true, deepdown desire was connectedness. The *want* with which she had always fulfilled her need was through marriage, but here's the secret: Our wants are interchangeable!

"So, what, I'm supposed to just pretend to be insightful and chipper for these women? I'm supposed to act like I'm all better and have good advice to give them?" she asked me. "Because that doesn't feel right. That doesn't feel real."

"Good!" I said. "If you want to change your neuroprogramming, it's going to feel uncomfortable. It's okay to feel inauthentic when you adopt new positive changes, because you are creating new neuroplasticity. Just go fake it 'til you make it."

She reluctantly agreed, and I couldn't wait to see what happened for her over the course of the coming weeks and months. Raquel was about to embark on a journey that could change her life—by stretching beyond her established routines, by changing her schemas, and by creating new neuroconnections, she would be living life from a new vantage point.

THE PASSION OF A 3-YEAR-OLD

If only we could all live like 3-year-olds.

Have you ever really watched a 3-year-old? I can tell you one thing, if you ever see a bunch of them at a park, you're never going to see them sitting around saying, "Man, I am so bored. We did the slide three times and I'm done."

Three-year-olds at a park are like bees around a picnic table. They swarm and buzz. Three-year-olds don't even know how to walk—that slower pace comes later in life—they're either standing still or running.

Nobody messes with 3-year-olds, either. If you get into an argument with one, good luck. These little people do not compromise. They approach every disagreement with an unmatchable level of conviction and certainty: "Listen, I'm going to fight you until I fall asleep or I die, whichever comes first." It's exhausting, but it's hard not to be a little impressed with their ability to demand total fulfillment of their desires when we are so used to giving in when the fight gets hard.

For us grown-ups, what is better than sleep? When we get up in the morning, it's painful. It's emotionally draining. It's like we are breaking up with our pillow. We get up and look back at our bed with tears in our eyes, saying, "Bye, bed. I'll miss you so much. This weekend, it's just me and you. I'm canceling all my plans and we're going to be together all day."[7]

A 3-year-old's biggest enemy is the bed. Children wake up in the morning like they've been shot from a cannon. They're excited and energized. Five a.m.: "I'm up! Mommy, *I'm UP!*"

How come 3-year-olds are unbeatable and unstoppable?

What's their secret ingredient?

It's one word: transparency.

Three-year-olds are too young and emotionally undeveloped to be self-aware. They don't get embarrassed by failure. They don't wait for your approval. They don't question their self-worth if another kid doesn't play with them. They don't care about the social ramifications of not sharing what they perceive to be theirs. They say what they want. They laugh and cry at a moment's notice. They are fully transparent. What you see is what you get.

Their goals may seem insignificant to you, but when 3-year-olds see something they want, they go after it. They don't care how they look. They don't care if you are mad at them. They have one focus: the cookie, the toy, the iPhone, whatever it is.

In fact, that's pretty much how we are from ages 2 to 5. That's where it all happens. When you hit 2, you can't do much, but by the time you get to 5, you've learned every basic life skill. You can walk, talk, eat, go to the bathroom—all you need after that is some math and vocabulary and you're good to go!

How do they grow so much in such a short period of time?

When you live with that much freedom, you live with every fiber of your being. No internal contradictions, no long bouts of guilt and introspection. No grudges. No regrets. You attack the world with enthusiasm and energy. The world is yours.

Three-year-olds grow and learn, strive and excel, not because they go to the right schools or have the right training. It's because they have the right mindset.

So what happened? Why did we ever give that up? We're born with this ability to stare at a challenge and overcome it, so how did we go from wanting to grow and accomplish to losing that luster, courage, and resilience?

For that matter, each of us was born as a unique puzzle piece. We didn't want to conform. We didn't want to listen. We were each our own worlds. And according to every 3-year-old, the world needs to adapt to *them*.

When did that change?

THE BIRTH OF THE IMAGE

It happens to my children (and according to research, many others as well) around 7 or 8 years old.[8]

It's winter and I am putting them on the school bus. It's cold outside, so I put on their hats, jackets, gloves, and knapsacks. This routine worked well for a long time, on every cold morning we had, but then one day something changes. My 7-year-old turns around and hands me back the hat. I say, "No, honey, put your hat on, it's cold outside." "I'm not wearing my hat, Daddy," she says. "How come? You're going to get sick." "Yeah, but if I wear my hat, I'm going to look like a . . . geek!"

Somewhere in the micro-society of the second grade, my child was taught to think, "Although it may cause my body physical harm, there is something far more important to worry about, my image. I may be cold, but that's better than not fitting in with my friends."

In that moment, the child stops purely wanting to grow, to change, to strive for greatness, and instead starts worrying about how he or she looks in the eyes of others. Being great is replaced with looking great, and looking great is no longer a matter of personal opinion. They think, "There's something else out there, and we need to conform to *that*. We need to be like others." And it's in that transition we start to convince ourselves that what we really want in life is not greatness, but acceptance. We want approval.

We start believing that we are not as valuable as we once thought. So we stop trusting ourselves. We stop believing in ourselves. We develop our insecurities.

And this happens while our peers are going through the same thing. Suddenly *everyone* is focused on themselves.

When you start to become self-aware, you live with two identities: the real you and your image, the you that everyone sees. At first, your image just covers you. It helps you navigate social environments. But over time, it controls you. You start to act, say, talk, and analyze life based on what is good for your image rather than your true self.

The transparency of the child starts to grow opaque. This is more than a substitution of your goals. It's not just collecting symbols to feel significant. This isn't about accomplishing. This is a substitution of self. We are not trying to *beat* the group; we are trying to *be* the group. We are not looking to stand out to feel significant, we are looking to fit in, to be connected. In fear that people won't connect to who we really are, we offer them a version of what we think they want us to be.

SETTLING FOR ATTENTION

We have a spiritual need to connect to others, to have authentic relationships. Should we feel alone, we experience a deafening emptiness. So we begin our lives trying to get the love of the people around us: our parents, our grandparents, our siblings. That love, especially when we are little, is usually easy and genuine. As we get older, we look for that connection to people outside the initial circle, but soon realize that love is hard because the people around us don't love us, they love themselves.

So in an effort to feel something, we give up on love, on a *real* connection, and settle on something more self-focused: attention. Attention (not to be confused with focus, as we discussed in Chapter 4) is the counterfeit to love. It's the equivalent of the material pleasure to a spiritual need.

When you go to a rock concert and see all these people screaming "We love you!" they don't actually *love* the band. They love themselves in that moment. They love how the music makes them feel and the connection to others who feel the same way. If the band would stop playing, they would stop loving. The front man turns to the guitarist and says, "Hey man, they love us!" because he thinks that what he feels is love.

However, it is not love. It's *attention*. Love is a relationship in which both parties are giving; attention is a relationship where one or both parties are *taking*.

So we grow up, and while we yearn for real love, we often stop seeking it out. We settle instead for attention, which is easier to sense and to grasp. From that first settling, our neurological connections toward seeking attention (instead of love) become stronger and stronger, until they become automatic. Soon enough, we dress, talk, walk, and act in a way that will get the attention we seek, even if that attention doesn't reflect our true selves and doesn't come close to satisfying the needs we feel in our soul.

As we grow up, we become very aware of what gets people's attention. One day, you make a wisecrack and people laugh. You start realizing that being funny is connecting you to people, so you become the class clown. Or people feel sorry for you. You start to realize that hurting yourself gets attention, so you start engaging in destructive behavior or acting depressed.[9] Or you wear something and everyone looks, so you start dressing only with the intention of getting more people to look at you.

The problem comes when we never outgrow this. We just up the stakes. We turn to Botox and plastic surgery to look younger than our years. We fall for get-rich-quick schemes or borrow beyond our means to purchase things to appear wealthier than our net worth.

None of that leads to a real human connection, because the one making the connection is not the true us. It's our image. And the image is not real. For someone to fall in love with your image, or for you to fall in love with the image of someone else, is not real. It's not authentic. In fact, for so many, we don't even know who the real us is anymore. We have been controlled by our image for so long that when we relate to other people, that person is not *us*. What was once a transparent self that easily connected to everyone around us and only had genuine relationships is now an opaque cover searching for attention, protecting our image, and blocking the spiritual energy that is inherent in real human connection.

Just like the symbols of significance that play as the trap to true significance, attention is the trap to true connectedness. We feel attention much quicker than we feel love because it's instantly gratifying, because attention is coming *to* us while love is something that we're *giving*. Love is more subtle. And it comes after lots of sacrifice.

We're trapped because attention only feels good while we're getting it. When someone turns their eyes away, we immediately feel it, unlike with love which remains long afterward. We're trapped because we have to keep upgrading the attention in order to maintain the baseline. Ask anyone how they felt the first time 20 people liked their selfies on Instagram and they'll tell you they were over the moon. Ask that same person 5 years later, when they have 10 times as many "followers," and they'll tell you that 20 "likes" is disappointing.

So how can we break free from these traps? How can we get to true love and connectedness in our lives? One of the easiest ways to begin to do this is to go back to the same method we used in order to get to the notion of true significance in our lives: Recognize your mortality in order to find your true self.

THE TWIN TOWERS EXERCISE

In the last chapter, I mentioned the resiliency and connectedness New Yorkers shared in the wake of 9/11.

At Thanksgiving dinner on that November 2001, I sat across the table from a woman whose husband was in one of the towers when the planes hit. We were all going around the table, sharing things we were thankful for, and she was clearly upset when the turn came around to her. None of us expected her to speak. But she did. And as she spoke, everyone at the table listened.

She and her husband had gotten into a fight that September morning. Without so much as a good-bye, he went off to work and she went to run her carpool duties with the children. When she came home after drop-off, she saw the red light flashing on her answering machine. She figured it might be her husband calling to apologize, but she ignored it and turned on the television to catch her favorite morning show. Only her show wasn't on. On her TV screen, she saw the images that are now burned into so many of our memories: the Twin Towers on fire, the black smoke streaming into the blue September sky.

Her husband worked in the South Tower.

She turned the volume up, trying desperately to understand what was happening. Trembling, and with tears in her eyes, she walked to her answering machine. She pressed play. The voice on the machine was her husband's. As the tower collapsed to the ground in front of her eyes on television, she listened to her husband's voice. He said he was sorry. He told her that he loved her. He told her that she was the greatest thing that ever happened to him.

In the few seconds he had left on this earth, the only thing that mattered to this man, the one thing he wanted and needed to do, was to tell his wife that he loved her. And she was thankful for that on that Thanksgiving Day. She was thankful for her husband's words and his love, and only wished that she could have had the chance, even a few seconds, to tell him the very same words herself.

A few days later, I shared this story with my college students, and I asked them: "What would you do if you were in that man's situation? Who would you call?" I asked them to get out a piece of paper and write down "Who would you call?" and "What would you say?"

I didn't ask them to actually call anyone. I just asked them to think about it. But right after class, a whole bunch of those students immediately went off and called someone they cared about, to tell them that they loved them. It was stunning to me. Just the thought of putting themselves in that man's shoes left them wanting to act on their feelings.

I've told that story in many of my classes and conferences ever since. I call it the Twin Towers Exercise, and I am amazed that even after all these years, the majority of people end up making those phone calls and telling someone important in their lives just how much they mean to them.

I want you to do a Twin Towers Exercise right now. Picture yourself in the Twin Towers as the plane hits underneath you. You've only got one call left. One call. Who do you call? And what would you say? Be free with your thinking. You don't have to actually make the call. Don't let fear, or emotional discomfort, keep you from writing down what's in your heart. Write it out. Who do you call, and what do you say?

Every one of us has at least one relationship that could be completely changed with a single conversation. One conversation with that old high school friend you haven't spoken to in 20 years because of one immature misunderstanding; the son you never praised and who every day carries the baggage of thinking that his parent isn't proud of him; the mother you hurt with your words back when you were an irrational teenager; the wife who doesn't really know how much you love her, even though you're living with her. Making that one phone call could transform your relationship forever.

Why don't we make these calls?

Tragedy could strike at any moment. So why don't we live this way all the time? Why aren't we fully transparent with the people who mean the most to us?

SHAME

We all seem to carry an irrational fear of leaving our emotional safe zone, and for this reason, we don't tell our loved ones how we really feel about them. It makes no sense, of course, because sharing true feelings is how you build relationships. If you communicate authentically, your relationships flourish. But because everyone has a comfort zone, most would rather say something inauthentic or say nothing at all rather than leave that comfort zone.

Why?

Because we lost that passion of the 3-year-old.

When you are comfortable being the real you, not only do you better connect to people, you also become more alive, vibrant, and fearless.

Serving an image is exhausting. Making sure you gain people's attention is tiring. And most importantly, as you become more self-aware, you start to hear a voice whispering to you, reminding you, "You are not enough." You're not successful, smart, attractive, rich, kind, or generous enough. And, you believe that voice. You think, if I am not enough, then I can't share the real me with anyone else because they will see that and want to leave.

Brené Brown said it best in her famous TED Talk.[10] She articulated this feeling in one word: shame. Shame is the fear that there is something about us that, if other people know it or see it, will make us unworthy of connection.

Brown posits, based on years of research, that not only do we all experience shame, but that the people who *don't* experience shame lack capacity for human empathy or connection. Think about it: She's saying that if you are an emotionally healthy human being, you should feel some measure of "I'm not enough."

But how much? That deep-down feeling of not being worthy enough breeds an insecurity that weakens us and causes us to pass up moments of genuine connection. It makes us present ourselves through our opaque image and not our true selves. It causes us to miss opportunities for real human connection, ensuring that we don't leave our comfort zone, just to make sure that we "look good."

The thing we have to realize is that people with great relationships aren't more worthy than me and you. They aren't more special. They don't have better genes, talents, or traits. They don't experience love and belonging because of the feedback from the people around them. They feel the connection because they push themselves to be vulnerable. They don't let shame hold them back. They allow their inner 3-year-old to shine. They make the call before disaster strikes.

They give, and then they feel worthy. They love, and then they feel valuable. They come out of their comfort zone to make someone else feel loved or special, and then they feel connected.

Giving requires us to be vulnerable, which is hard. And as Brown articulates, "Vulnerability is the core of shame and fear in our struggle for worthiness, but it is also the birthplace of joy, of creativity, of belonging, of love."[11] It's the willingness to make the Twin Towers call even when you hope that you'll get the voicemail. It's the confidence to say what you feel even if it's not reciprocated. It's the courage to be you, even if you think people want your image.

We all want connection. We need connection. But it starts with vulnerability.

Vulnerability breaks the hold of our image. Attention is the opposite. Attention comes from designing the perfect picture of yourself and sharing it with everyone so they can "like" it. Vulnerability admits we're broken, we're human, we're flawed. And when you act under the concept of "I may not be worthy, but I'm going to reach out anyway" or "I'm as worthy as I am, and I'm comfortable with that," *that* is how you connect. That's how you give the greatest gift you have: yourself. And only through giving will you connect to your spark, to others, and to Unified Energy.

True connection is not becoming successful. True connection is becoming real. And that is very different. Through the process of becoming vulnerable and authentic, you're able to break the trap of attention and be the real you again—and only when you're real can you really connect to other people. This is true with marriages, friendships, parents, coworkers, every single type of relationship in our lives. We don't have to be perfect. We just have to be us.

Want to test it? Want to see if you're up for it? If you're ready to give? Go ahead and make the Twin Towers call. Right now. Set this book down and make the call to one person you love, simply to let them know how important they are in your life. It doesn't have to take long. And even if you feel a knot in your stomach, embrace it. That vulnerability is good!

In fact, if you want to make this exercise even stronger, specifically pick someone in your life with whom you've never been totally honest and open, who has never seen the real, vulnerable *you*. Embrace the feeling. Pick up the phone. Get over that fear, which is based entirely on your image, and take this first step toward improving the connectedness in your life.

That one call, which digs down to your authentic self and opens you up to true connectedness, could very well be the spark that sets everything else in motion.

RAQUEL'S RESOLUTION

Raquel followed through on her homework. She found some support organizations for divorced women in her area and volunteered to help in any way she could.

After months of corresponding via e-mail, she called me. I hardly recognized her voice. Over the course of just a few months, working with those organizations and support groups and becoming a mentor to other divorced women, Raquel had completely changed.

"You were right," she said. "I thought because my marriage was gone, I had nothing left to give. But I did. I had a lot to give. A lot. I just needed to give it."

Her voice was full of hope and promise. She sounded younger. She no longer sounded broken, because she wasn't. She was whole again.

Raquel was able to create deep relationships with all sorts of people by using her pain as a source of giving. She found new friendships with coworkers at those organizations and created unexpected bonds with women of all ages who'd experienced a similar loss. Through those friendships and the work she did, Raquel regained a sense of connectedness that was much broader than any she had ever known in her marriage, along with a sense of significance she had never known in her life.

Her days were full. Her nights were full, too. She stopped calling friends and family to complain. She found she had some valuable advice to share with others after all—life lessons born of all sorts of struggles throughout her many years of marriage that would help to guide some of the other women to find happiness again and do it a lot quicker than she had.

By doing all of this, Raquel changed her neuroconnections. By shifting her attention from wallowing in grief to giving to others, her brain started to create new neuroconnections that brought her more happiness. Over time, it started to shift her schema, and she approached her day differently. She looked out into the world and saw new methods for giving and connecting and a new hope for the future.

When she allowed herself to be vulnerable to these new women, she found connection through the realness. She didn't have to be perfect or have it all figured out. She just had to be real. She grew stronger by being more vulnerable, by reaching out to other people who needed her help and sharing her story.

In time, she was able to be there for her children again, too—not as the sad mom who wanted to remind them how their father had hurt her, but as the vibrant and wiser mother who was now standing on her own two feet, with new purpose and direction in life.

"I don't feel like a burden to my children anymore," she told me. She laughed after she said those words. "I think they actually want to be around me."

I kept in touch with Raquel off and on after that. I saw her the next time I was in her part of California and barely recognized her when she walked in the room. She stood tall. She walked with confidence. She looked 10 years younger, but not in a phony way. She just looked more vibrant because she *was*.

A few years later, Raquel called me right after the holidays. She had managed to build bridges back to every one of her family members, and she'd thrown a huge holiday party at her home. All of her kids and their spouses were there, and so was one other very special guest: her ex-husband. She'd managed to build a bridge wide enough to allow him back into her life, for the sake of their children.

It turned out her ex's relationship with the coworker didn't last. He moved on rather quickly to another younger woman, and that relationship flamed out too. Raquel was most amused that her ex wouldn't leave her alone the entire night. He was completely enthralled by the woman she had become. He kept complimenting her on how great she looked and how much younger she seemed. Raquel laughed because she was no longer interested in him.

While he had gone through two short-lived relationships with much younger women, each time convinced that he'd found love when in fact all he'd found were relationships based on taking, she had spent that time maturing, evolving, deepening herself—growing in every way.

Years after her world had collapsed around her, Raquel realized that the cycle she was in, a cycle that could have destroyed her, had actually made her become a better person. All it took was properly tapping into the need for connectedness, as opposed to living and breathing the negative cycle of attention.

Sometimes it takes time to realize that even the hardest moments can be a blessing. But Raquel is living proof that it's possible. Once you learn how to use the control of your mental dashboard to access your spiritual needs, anything is possible.

LIVING WITH BOTH

While significance and connectedness are the fundamental needs that can put you on the path to a deeper satisfaction in life, those needs are also the root of pain for many. They're the hunger that drives people to the microwave. The yearning to fulfill these inner needs is what drives us to the traps: We settle for the symbol or the attention, because we either don't know of another way to satisfy our spiritual needs or are scared to push past the material for the metaphysical, the synthetic for the authentic. We settle, not because we don't want to live more meaningfully, but because we don't have faith in ourselves that we will find what we are looking for.

But it goes one step further. There is still a hurdle to overcome, and that is the balance of the two key traits. Even if you are living with true significance, there is part of you that wants and needs a real relationship with someone. There are those who spend their time solely focused on connectedness. They have deep and meaningful relationships with their spouses, children, and relatives, but they are left feeling as if they could contribute more to the world.

Neither one of these scenarios is fulfilling by itself. We need both significance and connectedness in order to live full lives. We need to feed both of those energies in order to feel spiritually complete.

Just like with any machine or organism, the parts may have

separate functions, but it is only when they're working in harmony that we see the vitality and the effectiveness of the whole. Think of all the integrated moving parts that make a Ferrari roar or a minivan so functionally perfect for a growing family. Or when a dancer is dancing, it's only when the arms, legs, hands, feet, heart, lungs, and brain operate in unison that the whole becomes greater than the sum of its parts. So, too, when you are able to tap into a healthy significance of self that is complementary to your connectedness to others will you tap into the energy that makes everything work, grow, move, blossom, or even explode.

The good news is, as we saw with both Dave and Raquel, most people find that once they're aware of their innate needs and have some clue about how to satisfy them spiritually, the pursuit of one often leads to a fulfillment of the other. They go hand in hand. And when you're connecting to Unified Energy, when you're achieving deep connections through giving, that energy flows to all the areas of your life. That's why Dave, who was deeply connected to significance, was able to find connectedness; and why the 3-year-old, whose transparency breeds authentic relationships, is able to accomplish so much, so fast.

And let's not forget that neither Dave nor Raquel considered themselves "spiritual" people and yet they were able to benefit from this ancient wisdom. Dave and Raquel were able to change because they used the power of the mind to help feed the needs of the soul.

Dave was finally able to see what true significance was all about because he was able to create new neurological connections that made it easier for him to do so. By shifting her perspective and attention toward new things, Raquel changed her neurological wiring through the power of neuroplasticity and now relates to the world in a way that fulfills her deeper spiritual needs.

Change your focus, change your schema, and harness the power of neuroplasticity to change your mind. That's how it works. For both Dave and Raquel, shifting their beliefs and their attention enabled them to break free of the issues holding them back.

What's amazing to me is that the very same principles apply across the board. Using the power of neuroplasticity to help us satisfy our most fundamental needs actually works. I've seen people who were addicted to alcohol and drugs use these principles to kick their addictions once and for all. I've seen people who struggled with weight for years suddenly turn their lives around and not only get thinner, but healthier and more driven in other areas of their lives. Once you identify your spiritual needs and leverage how your brain works, *you* control where you go.

Is it an easy fix? No. Is it a quick fix? Not necessarily. Greatness has been and always will be difficult. Dave and Raquel's transformations didn't happen overnight, but only with weeks and months of persistence and resilience.

What I'm telling you, what science is telling you, what spirituality is telling you is it's possible.

It's all there inside of you. You just have to unlock it.

So how can you apply these principles in your own life? What practical, realistic steps can you take to make your life the life you want?

The answers are found in Part III.

HOW TO MAKE THE IDEAL REAL

CHAPTER 9

THE SIMULATOR: NAVIGATE LIFE LIKE A SEAL AND A SURGEON

"I never hit a shot, not even in practice, without having a very sharp in-focus picture of it in my head."

—JACK NICKLAUS

Growth is hard. Change is scary. Transformation seems nearly impossible. That's why so few of us do it.

What makes lasting change so difficult is that it requires us to do two seemingly contradictory things simultaneously. On the one hand, in order to effect any real change, we need vision. We're stuck every day in the back-and-forth of life, and we need to see past our daily responsibilities—over the treetops, as it were—in order to know where we want to go.

On the other hand, we need to stay grounded and navigate the terrain. We need take action to make change. We need to adjust that same daily grind to take us to a new location.

Real change requires vision and action. Clouds and rocks. We need to see in the spiritual but implement with the physical.

We know ourselves. (Or at least, we think we know ourselves.) Some of us are great at vision. We can see 10 steps ahead but get exhausted at the thought of action. Others of us can execute all day but can't pick our heads up to see where to go. How many times have we said, "I'm going to change" or "It's going to be different"—and meant it—only to fail in the follow-through? Most of us have done it often enough to now assume that we are not really going to change.

Finding balance is the challenge: to let ourselves dream big, but then to practically implement the necessary steps to reach those new horizons.

Dave and Raquel didn't change because of one conversation. Our conversations may have started their journeys, but they changed because they executed. They took the time and put in the effort to gain both the vision and the action.

In Part II, we focused on delving deep into the soul. It wasn't "practical"—and that was on purpose. The point of going soul searching was to stop, step off the treadmill of our fast-paced lives, and gain perspective.

In Part III, we'll climb down from the treetops and discuss how to make the real, practical changes in our lives. And the way we do that is to begin with the underutilized power of visualization.

SEE LIKE A SEAL

Training to become a combat soldier is tough, but training to becoming a Navy SEAL is exponentially harder. The Navy SEALs are not just your everyday heroic soldiers. They are the best of the best. They've gone the extra mile—or more likely, the extra thousand miles. They've done the work to become masters of terrain and extreme conditions that the majority of people could never handle. They've trained to endure and overcome impossible situations in hostile territories, behind enemy lines, in total darkness, under water, in mid-air, and worse.

Out of the thousands of Navy recruits each year, only a small percentage get accepted to SEAL training—and only a small percentage of them actually graduate. There are currently 2,450 active-duty SEALs, which is just 1 percent of all Navy personnel.[1]

At one point, the passing rates were not just low, they were too low. The Navy worked hard to find the best recruits and invested considerable time and resources into them, leaving the leadership disappointed in the low graduation rate. They expected far more of these hand-selected recruits to make it through the program. In time, they noticed that they were losing good soldiers not because they couldn't hack it, but because a significant number of them had a mental block in one particular area of training: the water.

During SEAL training, the recruits go through a drill in a pool where they are forced to remain under water for 20 minutes. Equipped with oxygen tanks, their assignment is to just stay under water for the allotted period of time.

But there's a catch. The instructors jump in the water and harass the recruits during the drill. They rip off their masks, tie their air lines in knots, and punch the trainees in the gut, leaving them in the state of mind that would send any normal human swimming for the surface in a panic. But these aren't normal humans. Their job is to *not* panic, to wait until the attack is over, and to calmly fix the problems while remaining under water. Only once they make it through the entire 20 minutes are the recruits brought up to the surface by the drill instructors.

But the opposite often happens. Soldiers *do* panic, and even with four chances to pass at different points in the program, only 25 percent of recruits were making it.[2]

The SEALs weren't about to lower their standards. So instead, they turned to psychology for answers and began putting their recruits through a Mental Toughness Program, a training program designed by neuroscientists to control the SEALs' instinct to panic.[3] A key component of the program was doing a "mental rehearsal" before going in the water.[4] In a setting away from the pool, psychologists taught the recruits to visualize themselves in the water, getting harassed, and staying calm throughout the entire experience. Before they ever got in the water, the recruits envisioned themselves *not* freaking out, *not* panicking, steadily untying the knots in their air lines, and calmly dealing with the challenges for the entire time under water.

Something pretty remarkable happened. After the recruits went through one of these programs, which included a short period of time spent visualizing how they would handle themselves during that test, passing rates went up from 25 to 33 percent.[5]

If the real-life passing rate in one of the most rigorously challenging programs on earth could increase nearly 10 percent after a "mental rehearsal," can you imagine what would happen if we did the same before tackling our own endeavors?

We are all gifted with an imagination, an incredible capacity to see things that exist only in our minds. If we take the time to step away from our daily routines and, instead of jumping right into *doing*, start *seeing* the results we want to achieve, then our brains will enable us to perform at a higher level in real life.

How does it work? Why does it work? Why are the SEALs now graduating more recruits while keeping the drills as tough as ever?

It all goes back to neuroplasticity.

BACK TO NEUROPLASTICITY

Every time you have a thought, that thought triggers neurons, which form new neurological connections, restructuring your brain. As a child, I heard the word *ball* and learned to associate it with a round object. Between hearing the word *ball* and also thinking it, the connection between the word and the object became so strong that the word *ball* became automatic. Neuroplasticity 101.

The thing to remember is that I could have learned that word without ever having touched a ball. You learn all sorts of words without having physical contact or interaction with the objects or places those words describe. The truth is, you can learn almost anything without actually experiencing the subject. If you can think a thought, then your brain can create a connection around that thought. If you can visualize running a race and winning, then because of neuroplasticity, your brain will create new neuroconnections that will enhance your schema to include winning a race. You may not have stepped onto the track yet, but your brain already knows how to get to the finish line.

Now, you may not actually win. There's a lot of training and physical preparation that goes into conditioning a body to run faster than its competition. Visualization is not some sort of magic dream-fulfillment spell where you can think about something hard enough and get it. It's not that simple. But the fact is, building neuroplasticity around winning a race before you ever step foot on the track will get you much closer to winning than you might have thought possible.

OLYMPIC-STYLE VISUALIZATION

In a fascinating study regarding visualization in sports, Russian scientists compared four groups of Olympic athletes in terms of their physical and mental training ratios.[6]

Group 1 received 100 percent physical training.

Group 2 received 75 percent physical training and
25 percent mental training.

Group 3 received 50 percent physical training and
50 percent mental training.

Group 4 received 25 percent physical training and
75 percent mental training.

Guess which group showed the greatest improvement in performance?

Group 4. The group with the least amount of physical training performed the best. That's how significant the measurable effects of mental training are on physical performance. Visualization is not magic, but if used properly, it feels miraculous.

Robert Scaglione and William Cummins wrote about this in their book, *Building Warrior Spirit*:

> The Soviets had discovered that mental images could act as a prelude to muscular impulses. It has since become more widely understood and accepted in neuroscience and sports psychology that subjective training can cause the body to respond more favorably to consciously desired outcomes.[7]

Those studies showed the power of neuroplasticity in action. The subjective training that goes through your mind can actually change how you act and how your body performs.[8]

But the power of visualization goes even further. You can actually strengthen your muscles without doing any physical workout at all. Research has shown that mental practices can be almost as effective as true physical practice.

Guang Yue, PhD, an exercise psychologist from Cleveland

Clinic Foundation in Ohio, has made a practice of comparing "people who went to the gym with people who carried out virtual workouts in their heads." In a 2004 study, Yue and his fellow researchers focused on small muscles in the hand used in common daily activities and studied three groups of subjects.[9]

One group worked out those muscles 5 minutes a day, 5 days a week over the course of 4 weeks. They contracted their left pinkies 15 times with a 20-second rest between each, thereby exercising a group of three muscles of the palm that control the motion of the little finger. This group showed a 30 percent increase in little-finger muscle strength.

At the same time, Dr. Yue had two additional groups just *think* about doing that workout. The first group spent the same amount of time (5 minutes per day, 5 days a week for 4 weeks) thinking about working out their muscles. They saw a 13.5 percent increase in muscle strength. The third group didn't just think about working their muscles generally, they focused on the actual repetitions, including contracting their pinkies and resting in between. Some also imagined a voice yelling "Harder! Harder!" during the thought exercises. That group saw a whopping 22 percent increase in pinky muscle strength.[10]

How could this possibly be? How could you build muscle just by thinking about the exercises? The same question could be asked regarding any sort of mental-physical training: How can you run quicker just by thinking you can run quicker? How can you sink more baskets just by thinking you're going to sink more baskets? How could your mind change your performance?

The answer is: What makes you do *anything* is your mind, and your mind responds to the stimulus you send it. When you perform an action, your mind strengthens the neuroconnections that your body needs to complete the activity. That connection gets stronger and stronger the more you practice. But thoughts produce the same mental instructions as actions. Your mental imagery can impact as many cognitive processes in the brain as action, which means that the brain is training for actual performance during visualization.[11] This is much more than self-motivation or believing in yourself. You can actually increase your strength, accuracy, and capacity just by "mentally rehearsing."[12]

But it goes further. The stimulus you send your mind—stimulus that you can control—can impact not only your physical strength, but also your capacity to deal with life. It can help you better handle pressure and stress, enable you to adapt to unexpected scenarios, and allow you to access critical information when it's time to present a speech or close a deal.

Typically, your mind learns by experience. That's the value of experience: Once you've done something, your mind has "been there" before and can help you to navigate a better path the next time around.

But science is showing us that we don't have to wait for the experience. All experience is really memory. It is the product of neuroplasticity. So why wait for actual events to create new neuro-connections? If we imagine acting in a successful manner, our brains don't distinguish between envisioned images and those based on actual experiences. The mind doesn't like inconsistency, so if you can mentally visualize what you want to achieve and persist with that image long enough, then your mind will be primed to deliver it, regardless of the external factors around you.

You can acquire new schemas by just imagining them. You can develop neuroconnections from your couch. You can spur changes in your brain without having to go through the physical pain. If you can visualize it, you can start the process of making it happen.

YOUR OWN FLIGHT SIMULATOR

This means that you have the power to create a simulator for your mind—like a flight simulator—and teach it how to act upon your desires. You can show it what excellence looks like, so when you get closer to a challenge or you have to make a difficult decision or you need that mental toughness not to quit, your brain will already know what to do.

Your ability to create your own simulator enables you to reprogram your mind for *anything*.

For an example of visualization in action, let's look at Natan Sharansky. Growing up in the USSR, Sharansky was a chess prodigy who dreamed of one day being a world champion. At age 15, he became the champion of his native town in Ukraine.

What seemed like a promising career was abruptly cut short in his late twenties, when Sharansky was accused of spying for the United States. He spent nine years in prison, at times in solitary confinement. He decided to make good use of his time. While in solitary confinement, where he couldn't even read or write, he decided to play chess in his head. "Thousands of games," Sharansky later said. "I won them all." He visualized every move and countermove, sometimes more than one game at a time.

In 1996, 10 years after getting out of prison, Sharansky beat world-champion chess player Garry Kasparov. He attributed his win to the work he'd done in prison. Through visualization, he was able to hone the skills required to beat the world's greatest chess champion, in real life.[13]

But it doesn't have to take years to make visualization work. You can turn on your mental simulator each morning and visualize what you want to accomplish during the day.

Take Charlie Wilson, MD, DSc, former chairman of the Department of Neurological Surgery at the University of California, San Francisco, and one of the greatest neurosurgeons of the last century. A man who in his career routinely performed 15 brain operations a week and continued operating, sometimes up to five surgeries a day, into his seventies. He was an expert at one of the most delicate and life-threatening brain surgeries, the aneurysm repair.[14]

Wilson used visualization before every single surgery. He would mentally review every aspect of the operation ahead of time in what he called a "virtual rehearsal," so when he was in the operating room, he felt as if he were performing the surgery for a second time. In his mind, he had been there before and knew where he was headed. Should anything go wrong, he'd be able to handle it without panic, because he already thought everything through—kind of like a Navy SEAL getting ready to jump into the water.

One time, Wilson said, he completed a brain surgery and was already down the hall from the operating room when he realized that the virtual rehearsal and the actual operation didn't match. So he turned around, went back in, and discovered that there was a little remnant of tumor he didn't catch. He removed it, saving the patient's life.

USING THE SIMULATOR

Most of us are not brain surgeons. Most of us don't spend years in solitary confinement thinking about chess, either. Most of us don't dedicate our entire lives to training for the Olympics or have anywhere near the fortitude to join the Navy SEALs.

So how can we apply the power of visualization in our own lives? What can we do to make these techniques work for us in the here and now?

Before we leap into using visualization for bigger things like creating a better life, let's start with visualizing the completion of everyday tasks. Take a moment to think about an opportunity coming down the pike, a challenge you're up against, or a desire you want to fulfill. How much time have you spent worrying about what the outcome will be?

The anxiety we feel before we have to perform at a high level not only is detrimental to us emotionally, but also wastes precious mental energy that can be utilized for putting us in a better position to succeed.

Instead of fretting, visualize the most impactful way you should act and the results you want to achieve. If you can mentally walk through the necessary actions beforehand, you'll build neurological connections that you can draw on when you are actually in that situation. Here is the key: Don't just visualize the results, visualize the process. This is called process-based visualization, and from the SEALs to Sharansky to Wilson, people who effectively use visualization, mentally simulate the actions necessary to successful perform their tasks.[15] This enables them to not only achieve a higher level of performance, but to also better handle the stress, maintain focus, and persevere when there is an unexpected challenge or obstacle along the way.

Stop what you are doing for a few minutes and take the time to picture a task that will happen today. Then try to visualize the details in each step, and see yourself acting in the best possible way throughout the entire activity. By doing so, you are building neuroconnections that you can access later on when you are in that circumstance. Of course, it takes time for those connections to be strong enough to feel automatic, but you have to start somewhere. I use (and teach) these techniques all the time, especially when it comes to public speaking.

CLOSING OUT THE CONFERENCE

A few years ago, I delivered a keynote presentation at a business conference in Florida. The talk centered on the concepts we've been discussing, including the power of our beliefs, the impact of our schemas, and some of the strategies I'll be talking about in upcoming chapters. I finished the presentation and went back to my hotel room, ready to relax. I'd been on the road all week and was excited to kick back, finish some e-mails, and just enjoy the sun on my last day before heading home to chilly New York.

About an hour after I got to my room, I got a call from the front desk saying that the coordinator of the event wanted to see me. I was worried. Had I offended someone? It felt like I was being called to the principal's office in school. (Don't you hate that feeling?)

It turned out I wasn't in trouble at all. He said, "Listen, I liked what you had to say, but more importantly, I liked how you said it. Do you think you could coach me? I have to give the final presentation tomorrow, and I'm really nervous." So we got together after dinner to review his speech, and I gave him some public speaking techniques, which he probably already knew but needed a refresher on.

Somewhere around 5 a.m., my phone rang. It was him. "I'm sorry to call so early, but I'm really nervous. This is the first time I am closing a conference, and I'm afraid I'm going to completely blow this speech."

I realized that in all of my advice, I had forgotten the most important piece.

We met downstairs over coffee as the sun began to rise over the bay, and I explained to him the concept of visualization. I talked about neuroplasticity and the imagination and the research that showed how powerful "mental rehearsals" can be.[16]

Then I asked him to close his eyes and picture himself up on that stage. As the sun broke over the horizon and hit his face, I could see him wince at the very thought of it. He was terrified. It's amazing just how big a fear public speaking is for most people. As Jerry Seinfeld famously said, "According to most studies, people's number one fear is public speaking. Number two is death. Death is number *two*. Does that sound right? This means to the average person, if you go to a funeral, you're better off in the casket than doing the eulogy."[17] Speaking in front of others is one of the most nerve-wracking endeavors humans seem to encounter.

So I said to him, "Okay. I want you to do it again, but this time I want you to visualize yourself dealing with all of that nervousness, all of that fear, in the most empowering way possible. When you feel the nervousness, I want you to remember that *everyone* feels nervous. And when you get on that stage for the first time, I want you to see yourself stopping to take a deep breath, so you can start strong. And when you envision yourself delivering a joke and nobody laughs, I want you to see that you keep going anyway. You're going to speak slowly and not run through it, and you're going to pause and click through all the right slides. Go through every moment of the speech, all of it, in your mind, including how good you feel after delivering the speech you wanted to deliver."

He closed his eyes, and I could actually see him grow more empowered. He sat with confidence in his body, a smile coming to his face as he went through it in his mind. As we left, I said, "You're not speaking 'til noon. Go back to your room. Do it three or four more times."

I then ran to catch my plane, but promised I would follow up with him when I landed.

As soon as the wheels touched ground in New York, I texted him: "So?"

"It went better than expected . . . ," he replied. "But I still have a long way to go."

I texted back: "Welcome to life."

We've been in touch ever since, and his speaking abilities have grown exponentially. Why? In part because he's followed tips and techniques for becoming a better speaker. But equally important is that to this day, he never gives a speech without visualizing the entire speech first. He reviews all of the challenges in his mind and envisions coping with each of them. He puts himself in a position where his brain starts gearing him up for success long before he steps on the stage.

I've taught this style of process-based visualization to a wide variety of business leaders, community leaders, spiritual leaders, and various types of speakers, from the professor starting a new semester to the motivational speaker who is about to address his first really large audience. It works for everyone.

So I ask you to do the same, whatever it is that you do. Do you play a sport? Do you have stress at work? What performance are you not satisfied with? I want you to visualize doing it better.

I don't mean to just sit back and wait for the world to give it to you. Do the work that's needed. Prepare. Get ready. Go through all of the physical practice you need to put yourself in a position of excellence. But do the mental work, as well. Sit down, even if it's just for 10 minutes. Shut everything off. Set a timer on your phone, so you'll know when time is up. Close your eyes and walk through the entire event in your mind. Walk through how you're going to feel. Allow the feelings of negativity to come in, but then mentally see how you're going to deal with them. Put yourself in different potential scenarios and visualize how you are going to thrive in each of them.

Once you have begun to experience the results of visualizing the completion of daily tasks, you can begin to apply the technique to the deeper questions in your life. Visualization is a powerful way to experiment when you don't necessarily know exactly what you want. You can use it as a tool to figure out the answers to the bigger questions: Where is it that I want to go? What is it that I want to learn? What do I want my future to look like?

If you paid attention to what we discussed in Part II, then you have some idea of what the answers to those questions will be. What you really want to be aiming for are the things you need—including the satisfaction of your psychological needs and, most importantly, the fulfillment of your deep-rooted spiritual needs. But you may not know how to get there or even where "there" is.

To help figure that out, you need to begin to visualize your ideal self.

CHAPTER 10

CHISELING TO DAVID: THE PATH OF BE. DO. HAVE.

"The real me is not my body."

—CHRISTOPHER REEVE (AKA SUPERMAN)

Michelangelo was only 26 years old when he began work on David, his statue that would become one of the most widely recognized works of art in the world—a 17-foot-tall, 6-ton marble rendition of the biblical figure who took down the giant Goliath with nothing but a rock, a sling, the sheer force of his will, and his belief in God.

Notably, he created David from a piece of marble that was deemed unusable and had been discarded by two other sculptors. The work wasn't easy. Michelangelo barely ate or slept during the

3 years it took to complete, often falling asleep in an open court-yard with all of his clothes on—even his boots.

Originally commissioned by the Cathedral of Florence for its roofline, the statue was so instantly beloved that it was placed instead in a public square. What made the piece especially unique is that David had traditionally been portrayed as a victorious warrior. But Michelangelo chose to show David just *before* he fought Goliath—with his face concentrated, the slingshot and rock at his side in anticipation.

There is some dispute about this next part of the story, but after marveling at Michelangelo's statue, the pope reportedly asked the sculptor, "How did you know what to cut away?" Michelangelo's reply was, "I saw the angel in the marble and carved until I set him free."[1]

Visualization is like a chisel we use on ourselves to carve away that which weighs us down to reveal the masterpiece within. It allows us to remove the extraneous clutter in our lives so that we can find the inner David, which is nestled within each of us.

Yes, visualization can help you in your day-to-day life—to get better at your job, get over your fears, or get you more prepared for a task—but that's just scratching the surface. To really use it in its full power, we can use visualization to uncover our essential self.

Now, before we can visualize that, we have to contemplate what it means. How do we uncover our essential self? How do we know what it might look or feel like? With the constant noise and frenetic pace of our daily lives, how are we supposed to distinguish between who we really are and who society tells us we are?

The path to that level of personal discovery starts by creating a chasm between who you are and what you do, by recognizing the vast difference between being and doing.

BEING VS. DOING

What's the first question we ask when we meet someone? After their name, it's quite often "What do you do?" Whatever their answer is, we immediately think we have enough information to judge who they are. We make assumptions about how smart they are, how disciplined they are, how ethical or kind they are—all because of the answer to that one question about what they do, whether the answer is about their career or a hobby or even where (and if) they volunteer.

Sometimes we also judge people by what they have.

Have you ever met someone who seemed a little strange? They may dress really odd or conduct themselves in some manner that's outside the norm. As you try to figure them out, you find out that they are rich. Suddenly your assumptions change to, "Oh, they're just eccentric." You immediately find yourself respecting them more because of the fact that they have money, even if you don't know whether they earned it, inherited it, or stole it. *Having* it is enough to color your impression of who they are.

Maybe neither judgment is accurate, but we judge nonetheless based on what a person does and what a person has. Why? As we discussed earlier, our external environment has a very real impact on our schemas. Remember the elderly men in Ellen Langer's experiment or the high-scoring students in the Oak School experiment (both in Chapter 1)? The environment we are in has a profound impact on how we see ourselves.

In a world that doesn't have the means to understand the true essence of a person, we are stuck using other methods—ones that can be measured—to make assumptions about the people around us. So grades, awards, money, championships, net worth, or other symbols of success create the value of the person.

Society can't help itself. It has no other means to measure people. But that doesn't have to be what we use to measure ourselves.

Our personal worth should never be measured by what we do or what we have. Instead, it should be measured by who we are: our internal force, thoughts, and beliefs.

The fact is, there is a real risk in identifying with what we do and what we have. When we tie our identities to something outside of us, such as our careers, looks, or reputations, then we automatically remove ourselves from a position of control when it comes to our sense of self. The horrifying fact is that if any of these circumstances get taken from us—if we lose our jobs, fall out with a social group, or simply grow older and less attractive—we wind up losing much more than that circumstance. We wind up losing ourselves.

When your sense of self is rooted from within, nothing can take away the essence of what makes you, *you*. When we chisel deeper, we can develop a sense of identity that is independent from the ever-changing circumstances of the world around us.[2]

In order to do that, you need to recognize that you are a separate entity, independent of your job or your upbringing. You are not your body, and, if neuroplasticity has taught us one thing, you are not even your brain. You exist beyond those things, which is why you can gain control over all of them.

Finding your essential self is not something you stumble on in a moment of insight. It doesn't happen just to the lucky few, and it doesn't happen by chance. It's a process of self-discovery that we have been building throughout this book. It's difficult to separate what we do and who we are, and we will get into techniques for that. But for now, the simple recognition that *being* and *doing* are two separate things is absolutely critical.

THE FIRST STEPS OF CHANGE

Have you ever made a resolution only to realize that you made the same one the year before? You were sincere when you made it and may have really tried to implement it. But in the end, you regressed. Why?

Because you missed a step. You can't start with what you *do* (your actions) before you work on who you *are*. Your actions are the manifestations of your being. You can't try to change your actions unless you address the mental processes that cause you to act the way you do.

If you want to change your *do*, you first need to change your *be*.

Our actions are sourced by our identities. Unless we attack the root of the problem, we will keep on finding ourselves in the same place year after year. Changing what we do is short-lived, because what we do is being sourced by who we are.

By changing your identity, you will find a clearer path to changing your actions. Then the results will follow. By confronting and changing who you are, you will directly impact what you do.

To show how this works, let's go back to the topic of food. If you want to lose weight, you can start by resisting fatty or high-caloric foods. You can buy a diet program and promise to follow it strictly. You can join the gym and resolve to be there every day.

But more often than not, you quit. You binge and then don't go back to the diet routine. You stop going to the gym. You give up on the goal of losing weight or getting fit. That's just what happens, right? Almost every one of us has hit at least some part of this all-too-familiar cycle at one point in our lives. Gyms actually bank on the fact that you won't show up. Their memberships far exceed the space they have to accommodate everyone. They don't build gyms to fit all of their members, because they know that a large percentage of them will sign up but not show up.

The underlying reason why we can't stick to a gym schedule or a diet program is that we haven't focused on changing our identities. To our neuroprogramming, we are still a person who loves eating fast food and who, but for our waistline, dress size, or health issues, would still order the supersize burger and fries—with a Diet Coke, of course. That person, the one who values how food tastes over its nutritional impact, does not go to the gym. That person doesn't eat food that's green. So the person you are, the one who sees the world through a schema built from years of eating unhealthily, is constantly fighting the new actions you're undertaking.

While you attempt to change your *do* (diet, exercise), you haven't begun to work on your *be* (contemplating, realizing, and deciding that the real you is healthy). Your schema doesn't reflect an inner desire for health and wellness. So as long as you are feeling guilty, or overweight, or worried, you will force yourself to adapt to your new culinary habits—only to wind up sliding right back as soon as some other emotion overrides it.

That's why people eat terribly when they are stressed. Their schemas still view the world through the lens of an unhealthy eater, so when the stress of some crisis overwhelms the desire to look good and feel good, they hang up the phone and reach for the ice cream.

Changing your health starts with deciding who you want to be. Healthy eating, fitness, and wellness start in your mind, not your actions. You need to *want* to be a healthy person. You need to see health and wellness as part of who you are. Otherwise, you will always slide back in a moment of weakness or when the initial excitement wears off. Once you change your mentality, then you can ask yourself: What does a healthy person do? How do they eat? Do they exercise? How often?

When your actions are sourced from your being, it starts to become more natural and more resistant to your own preprogrammed pressures to maintain your previous habits.

If you think this sounds like a new concept, let me assure you it is not. Every first-time parent goes through it.

FIRST-TIME PARENTS

I remember when my first child was born. Before my wife gave birth, parenthood wasn't real. It was to her, of course. But to me? I think I was in denial about the whole thing. Sure her stomach grew, and I felt the kicking and the whining (from my wife, not the baby), but I didn't feel like a father.

A few hours after my son was born, it was the middle of the night and I couldn't sleep. My wife got the comfortable bed (something about having gone through labor), so I tried to sleep on a chair in the hospital room, but it just wasn't working out. So I walked into the nursery and found my boy.

As crazy as it sounds and as crazy as it must have looked, I started talking to him. I remember telling him that I had no idea what to do or how to raise a child. The sight of him overwhelmed me, and even though I didn't know so much as how to hold him correctly, I promised him on that first night that I was going to be a great dad. As I walked back to my wife's room, the promise I made to him resonated with me. I felt it. I had truly committed myself to being a great dad. Without realizing it, I had decided to change my *be*: By deciding to "be a great dad" and committing to that new identity, I was already moving my brain in the direction of helping me to figure out what to *do* about it.

I started to see the world with new eyes. For the first time, fatherhood was in front of me. My schema now enabled me to see the stimuli that was always there: information about what great dads do, how they act, how they balance their time with work, how they treat their children.

It's the same way I would later come to see young dads driving minivans once I gave in and started driving one myself. (Actually, that was a follow-through on being a "great dad," too. Great dads know it's more important to make mom happy than to drive the car you want.)

Our identities shift our schemas, which changes what is relevant. That enables us to take in new thoughts, which create new neurological connections. Over weeks, months, and years, those new neuroconnections about fatherhood became more habituated into my life. I learned how to feed, change, and hold my son. I became more tolerant of spit-up and of waking up at ungodly hours. I quickly began to consider his needs in every decision I made.

That's how change happens. *Be* leads to *do*, which ultimately leads to *have*.

The mistake so many of us make is we try to change what we have or what we do—thinking that once we've achieved something, then that will form our identities. We've been taught to think that the order of life is:

Do. Have. Be.

Do work. *Have* money. *Be* rich.
Do schoolwork. *Have* good grades. *Be* a great student.
Do parenting. *Have* a good relationship with kids. *Be* a great parent.

Do things, then *have* things, and that leads you to *be* something. This is how we see the world. The elements are correct, they're just out of order. How we should see the world is:

Be. Do. Have.[3]

If you make the decision to *be* something, it will open the door to seeing what that kind of person does, which, if you follow those actions, will lead you to have what that kind of person has. Being a great student leads to doing things that great students do (take notes, study, prepare), which leads to better grades. Being a great parent leads to doing the things great parents do (spend quality time, care, listen, help, support), which leads to a better relationship with your kids.

First, you have to decide to change your identity, your *be*. That shift will enable you to change what you *do*, and that will change what you *have*. As Zig Zigler once said, "You've got to be before you can do and do before you can have."[4]

JACKET AND TIE

I remember my first year as an associate at a large New York law firm. When I took the job, I made up my mind that someday I was going to be a partner in the firm. I didn't think of it as a pipe dream. I saw myself in that role. I just had no idea how to get there.

I tried to work as diligently as possible to impress my supervisors. I was paired up with a senior partner who was supposed to be my mentor. Yeah, right. I think I spent 10 minutes with him, once, as we were riding the subway on the way to a company event.

During my annual review, which he gave me, I asked him for a bit of advice on how to become a successful attorney. He gave me the strangest answer, which I immediately dismissed. Without even looking up, he said, "Wear a jacket and tie."

Jacket and tie? I thought. Some mentor.

I dressed business casual, which was the standard dress code in the office. I wasn't a male model, I was an attorney. I expected to be evaluated based on my professional capacity, not my personal style.

He moved on with my perfunctory review, and after a few minutes, I left.

I went home that night, though, and I decided that maybe I ought to try it. If that's all he had to offer for advice, and he was the one giving me my reviews, maybe I should give in and do it just to please him.

So for the next few months, I wore a jacket and tie to the office. At first, it didn't seem to make a difference. Then I started getting better and better reviews about my work. Not just from him, but from everyone. People started commenting on my attention to the details that others overlooked, my taking on additional responsibility, and the confidence I exuded at meetings with clients.

One day, I stopped in his office to check in. I told him that I wasn't sure if he had noticed, but I'd taken his advice to heart and started wearing a jacket and tie. "And," I said, "it seems to be working."

He smiled, satisfied that someone took his advice seriously. He sat back and then gave me the simplest but wisest explanation for my newfound success. "You know why it's working?" he said. "Because in today's corporate world, everyone dresses business casual. The only people that still wear jackets and ties are partners. Every day, when you look in the mirror, I wanted you to see yourself looking like a partner, so you would instinctively start to act like one."

I didn't realize I had been acting like a partner, but apparently to some extent I had. A very inexperienced partner to be accurate, but a partner nonetheless. Still, that made all the difference. When I walked into a room, I saw myself looking like one of the partners. I instinctively mimicked their actions and demanded of myself what they did. I didn't act like an associate, and I took responsibility for the cases like a partner would. My work reflected how I perceived myself. My *be* was influencing my *do*.

Dr. Ellen Langer did research on something similar. She studied people who routinely wear formal uniforms (UPS drivers, police, nurses) in their work lives and compared them to people who don't. She found that those who wear uniforms—clothing that does not change with age—missed fewer days to illness and had fewer doctors' visits and diseases, even though they had comparable socioeconomic status.[5]

Why would this be? As Dr. Langer put it, the changing styles of clothes we wear as we get older are a part of "the subtle signals that aging is an undesirable period of decline. These signals make it difficult to continue developing a healthy mindset throughout adulthood."[6]

Seeing yourself put on the clothes of an older person makes you feel older. Seeing yourself as "aging" leads to a decline in health. However, seeing yourself in the same work clothes you wore in your twenties lets your mind think you're not aging quite as quickly as your street clothes might let on.

This isn't a lesson in fashion, of course. It's the threshold of a much deeper concept.

Real change starts from a place of *being*, rather than *doing* or *having*. Like putting on a jacket and tie every day, once you decide who you want to be, you start to change your schema. There is a famous expression: "Dress for the job you want, not the job you have." It speaks to the same idea. I would take it a step further. Act like the person you want to be, not the one you *think* you are. When you do that, you start to see opportunities that were always there but you never saw before. You find strength you always had, but never tapped into. You see yourself doing things that you never thought possible.

Sensing these new opportunities leads you to act in new ways, which creates new neuroconnections in your brain, which, over time, makes those actions seem all the more natural.

When you start from *be*, you begin a process of reprogramming and re-creating your brain. Then something really cool happens: You start to get the things that a person of your new identity would have—not because of a gimmick, not because of some hocus-pocus, but because that's who you've become.

FREE TO CHANGE

I'm often asked in my classes and seminars, "Why is starting with *be* so important? Why can't we '*do have be*'? Why does it matter what order it's in? It's all part of the same thought process toward self-improvement, isn't it?"

The answer is that before you can make a change, you need to be *free* to change. True change cannot happen if we are saddled with thinking that our actions start the change. Actions don't start change; identity does.

Your *be* is independent of the current status of your body, your brain, and your neuroprogramming. Your *be* is free and unencumbered, which means it can change in a moment. You can read a book (like this one, I hope), realize something, and then make a decision to change your *be* instantly. And that change is real change. That change, if sincere and genuine, can enable you to broaden your schemas and see the world differently, to start a process of creating new neuroconnections and ultimately changing your actions.

Let me be clear: Executing on that decision may be quite a journey. It will take time. It will take a lot of doing, but making a change can happen in a moment. Once you see the world through the eyes of your *be*, your identity, you can take your life in any direction you want—even if the shift forces you to acquire completely new habits (while dumping the old).

How do we make that shift?

By getting our vision back.

YOUR IDEAL SELF

When we were younger, all we had was vision. We were unencumbered by reality and responsibility. Our future was brimming with possibility. We were going to be a hero. We were going to live life surrounded by beauty and love. We were going to be a basketball player, a police officer, a firefighter, and a doctor—all at the same time.

We went through school, and our vision started to diminish. We were tamped down by people—our parents, our teachers, even our peers—telling us: "Be more realistic." "Pick one thing." "Stay focused on the options we place in front of you." "Don't overreach."

Then we got out into the world and had to deal with reality, which meant we needed to get a job to pay our bills. Since most of our jobs are about fulfilling the dreams of someone else, we stopped dreaming about what we could be. The voices around us, and eventually the voices within us, said, "You can't be all of those things. You are not a kid anymore."

There is some truth in that. There is value in focus; in not staring out the window, dreaming of being somewhere else all the time; in taking responsibility and being a good citizen and a good worker. All of those things are good. They can be very satisfying, even at a spiritual level.

But if you want to change the course of your life, you have to start by seeing where you want to go. You have to get your vision back, to see what's possible, to see what's next.

Bestselling author and psychologist Daniel Goleman, PhD, said in his book *Primal Leadership:* "Connecting with one's dreams releases one's passion, energy and excitement about life. . . . The key is uncovering your ideal self—the person you would like to [be,] including what you want in your life and work. . . . Developing that ideal image requires a reach deep inside one's gut level. You know you have touched it when . . . you feel suddenly passionate about the possibilities your life holds."[7]

Being able to identify and visualize your ideal self unleashes the passion you need to make that version of yourself a reality. You need to see it, dig for it and feel it to have a chance of living it.

VISUALIZING THE IDEAL

The secret to creating an amazing future is to see it first; to dream, to soar, to remove the obstacles that prevent you from articulating your deepest desires; to introspect until you have the clarity of who you want to be.

Just to be clear: This is not, "It would be cool if . . ." Trying to articulate your ideal self is a mission worthy of pursuit if you want to live a great life.

Some of the great spiritual thinkers in history have encouraged us to take on this journey. In the midst of one of the greatest crimes humanity has ever known, one such spiritual leader, a rabbi, emerged.

As the Holocaust unfolded, and so much of the world fell into the despair of World War II, Kalonymus Kalman Shapira from Poland took it upon himself to inspire those around him. He was known to thousands of followers as a man whose wisdom was rivaled only by his courage. People traveled for miles just to hear his words and absorb in his insights, even while some of the greatest evil in the world was trying to hunt, round up, and eradicate Shapira, his followers, and all of those like him from the planet. He never gave up, and even after the Nazis killed members of his family and put him into an internment camp known as the Warsaw Ghetto, he continued to teach and share his light. He was later moved to a concentration camp and was killed by the Nazis on November 3, 1943.[8]

After the Holocaust, a manuscript was unearthed in which Shapira's followers had transcribed many of his pearls of wisdom. One such bit of advice was on how to change: "Each year, clarify a goal and envision the actualized 'you' of next year. Visualize who this 'you' will be: his attainments . . . his daily life . . . his character . . . and his inner essence. Use this envisioned 'you' as a gauge to know how far you still have to go. Is your present daily progress enough to create the reality of that envisioned future 'you'?"[9]

What's amazing to me is that Goleman, from the United States, and Shapira, from Poland, shared such a similar message. The reason that was possible, decades and thousands of miles apart, is because they knew this was a metaphysical pursuit. They knew that all of us, deep down, know who we want to be. We know our innate strengths. We know the subjects, activities, and interests that light us up when we engage in them. We also know those areas that we seem to be allergic to, the activities that drain us, and the pursuits that feel like the last thing we want to do.

It's the combination of recognizing those things that begin to make us *us*.

Goleman and Shapira are teaching us to break free of the shutdown of our passions—to reach into your ideal self with everything you have—because the vision and articulation of your ideal self is the first step to getting you closer to realizing it. And realizing your ideal self is what the journey of life is all about.

That's the key: uncovering that inner you that somehow got lost along the way, and then going after it.

Articulating your ideal self is not some nice thing to do when you have some free time. It's the very opposite. It is *essential* for your life.

Without the clarity gained by articulating your ideal self, even those who are already working to find their way toward greater life satisfaction may, in fact, be going in the wrong direction.

EXERCISE I: THE IDEAL DAY

Let's take the advice of Goleman and Shapira and attempt to visualize our ideal selves.

Set aside a block of time, at least 30 minutes, when you are least distracted—on a plane, in a coffee shop, at the office after everyone else has left, or at a quiet time in your house, maybe after the kids have fallen asleep.

Take out a sheet of paper, open your laptop, or use the chart on page 176. Pick a date in the future. Make it a specific date. It could be a year out, five years out, your 40th or 50th or 75th birthday, whatever you want. Find a date and make it specific. Then visualize yourself on that date in the future. Start to write out exactly what that day looks like, as if you are observing yourself, as if you were given a time machine to go to that date in the future and watch yourself. Really try, as if you're writing it as an observer, to get as much of that day—an *ideal day*—as possible.[10]

What is your schedule for the day? What time do you wake up in the morning? What do you have for breakfast? Who are you with? Where are you? What are you doing? What projects are you engaged in? What does your family look like?

Be as detailed as you can. You come downstairs to a certain breakfast, your house looks like this, these are the people at your kitchen table. Or maybe you're in a hotel. Or you're on a yacht. Anywhere you want to be! The key is to not be bound by your current constraints, although you do want to strike a balance of being realistically ambitious. If you go to complete unreality—say you want to be the queen of England—the exercise will be futile. But if you're too "realistic," then you're missing the point. Allow yourself to move to heights that are beyond what you normally think, beyond what you typically envision, but make sure there is at least some possibility of actually getting there, even if that possibility is remote.

What are you wearing? Where are you going? What do you look like? Use all sorts of details to map out your day.

Examples that I've received from people I've coached or taught, and even from myself include:

- "I woke up in the morning at 5 a.m. and jogged for 2 miles. I made a healthy breakfast. My wife came downstairs and together we got the kids ready for school. I walked my kids to the bus, and then put the finishing touches on my first book."

- "I leave my house and I go to the job I love. I'm a teacher, the best teacher in the district, and when I walk in the room, the kids erupt with excitement."
- "I'm a psychologist, and I've just finished giving a presentation to a conference on overcoming addiction. The audience, my peers, are very impressed and compliment me on the style and content of my presentation."
- "I am home with my family on Friday night, and we are just spending time together, and I have no other concern in the world. The family is around the table, laughing and enjoying the time together. No one is looking at their phones for the entire meal."
- "I run a large company and am up early in the morning. I grab my coffee as I walk outside to a waiting black car where I am whisked to the office, reading the *Wall Street Journal* and speaking on the phone with my COO." (It's funny that most people seem to be up early in the morning in their ideal lives. Maybe there's something to learn from that.)

Whatever jumps to mind when you consider an ideal day, write it down. Try to figure out how you make decisions. Try to get to what makes you happy. Try to think about the way people around you feel. (Notice similarities to your eulogy exercise.) Try to get as much of the picture of both your external environments and your inner thoughts and feelings throughout the day.

By writing down what we do on an ideal day, we're using a record of *doing* as a pathway to understanding our *being*.

It's important to actually write this out because writing has been shown to have a powerful impact on your brain. Writing down your thoughts creates stronger neuroconnections than just thinking. The act of putting ink to paper stimulates a part of the brain responsible for tactile learning called the reticular activating system (RAS). The RAS prioritizes what you are doing at any given moment and, when stimulated, lets other parts of the brain know, "This is important. Make sure to focus." (Studies show that typing is not as effective at stimulating the RAS as writing by hand, but it's better than just thinking about it.[11])

VISION

Date: ___, ___, 20___ [Date in future]
Some suggestions to get started
My eyes open and I look at the clock. It's ___ o'clock in the morning and . . .
My day consisted of . . .
I can't believe that its been __ years since . . .
I never would have dreamed that I am with . . . I am doing . . .

For a downloadable copy of this chart, go to charlieharary.com/book.

The first time I ever did this exercise was at a Starbucks. (Where would we do our deep thinking in the modern world if it wasn't for Starbucks?) I had a day off from work, and my house was way too noisy to think. I got there at 7 a.m., and I sat there with a Venti Sumatra, struggling to start the exercise.

At first, it felt weird and wasteful, like I was writing my own fairy tale that would never actually happen. I felt uncomfortable even writing certain things because they were way too ambitious and unrealistic. I stopped. I checked e-mail and social media. I looked around. I got up to get a refill. But I convinced myself that going *all in* on this exercise was worth 30 minutes of time. I promised myself I could get back to "real life" right afterward.

I restarted, and after 10 minutes or so, it felt incredible. Like I was free. As if every sentence could determine my future and make all my hopes and dreams come true. Once I got the ball rolling, I didn't stop typing for 2 hours.

The goal of this exercise is not to just throw your wish list to the universe and have it all come true. This isn't for the "universe," it's for you. This account of your ideal day is going to become the road map for your life. This will expose your deep-rooted dreams. This will reveal insights into your spiritual needs of significance and connectedness, and how to fulfill these needs in an authentic way. Your ideal self stems from your ideal day.

You'll know you've done this exercise well if, when you're done with it, you look at it and think, "If this was a day in my life, my life would be amazing!" If you're inspired by the very thought of what's written on that paper coming true, then you're getting there.

TAKING STOCK OF YOUR BE

Articulating your ideal day is just the first step. Once you've finished, go back and review it. Pay attention to what it reveals about who you want to be. The answers could be as mundane as "I want to be successful . . . " at a particular job, or as deep as a value: "I want to be somebody who always acts generously with others." Try to tease out how you know it's something you want to be. For example: How do I know I want to be loved by my wife and kids? Because on my ideal day, they are always around me. How do I know I want to be the greatest teacher? Because on my ideal day, I feel great because of my students. Ask yourself, "How do I know that I want to be rich? To be inspirational to others? To be an author?" all in the hopes of answering, "What are the things that I truly want to be?"

EXERCISE II: KNOWING YOUR BE

Below is a chart you can use. You have the ideal day from the previous exercise. Next to it, tease out all the things you want to be. Write down a simple explanation as to how you know that it's who you want to be.

VISION	BE	HOW DO I KNOW?
Your Ideal Day	A great parent	Throughout my day, I had my warmest moments with my kids. I allocated more time to them than I did my job or hobbies.
	An author	I can't imagine myself without a book.
	Generous with my money	I find myself involved in philanthropy throughout my day.
	Rich	My entire day was about financial success.
	Healthy	My food choices were healthy, and I saw myself as fit.

For a downloadable copy of this chart, go to charlieharary.com/book.

Then, if you want to go even deeper (which I hope you do), circle back to Part II and align what you want to be with your spiritual needs. Remember the difference between wants and needs and how our spiritual needs of significance and connectedness can be fulfilled through true connection (by giving) or through surface manner (by taking), through satisfying our spiritual spark or gratifying our material bodies.

Add a few more columns to your chart and check yourself to

see whether your be's are satisfying those innate needs in an authentic or counterfeit manner.

EXERCISE III: GIVING VS. TAKING

WANT	NEED	
BE	GIVING OR TAKING	HOW TO SHIFT IT
Healthy	Taking—want to lose weight to look good for others (Attention)	Giving—caring for my body so it can be healthy and productive (Significance)
Author	Taking—want to feel smart and get validation from others that I am accomplished (Attention)	Giving—want to inspire people (Connectedness)
Rich	Taking—want to buy whatever I want, to feel valuable and powerful (Materialism)	Giving—focus on giving my clients more value, which will increase my worth; want to provide for my family (Significance)
Great Parent	I want to give my children to have a great life (Giving)	N/A

For a downloadable copy of this chart, go to charlieharary.com/book.

Why is it important to do this? Because in your vision, you will see who you want to *be*. Your *be*'s are important to articulate because they are expressions of needs, and unless you come face-to-face with which desires you pursue to satisfy your inner needs, you may feel unsatisfied, even if you get what you want.

You need to understand what you want in life. Where is it coming from? Maybe you're trying to give, to grow, to add value. If so, great. But what if it's more selfish? Do you want that *be* because of an insecurity? Are you just looking for a way to take? It's okay if that's the case, just be honest with yourself. We are all a work in progress. In most cases, it's not black or white; it's probably a mixture of both selfless and selfish. Over time, we can evolve our *be*'s (remember that wants are interchangeable) and deepen our understanding of why we want certain things. That's what real growth looks like: It's gradual. Many times, our *wants* are selfish because we haven't ever spent time thinking about them. Once we do, we can work to make our lives more selfless.

Once you've done all of this, once you can see it all in front of you, you can start to make sense of it and move toward it—to begin the real journey. To go after it, fully, with your mind, body, and soul, by establishing a new set of rituals and habits that will lead you where you truly want to go.

By using the power of visualization to find your ideal self, you can create a road map for where to go to *be* that ideal self. And then? You can use the methods in the next chapter to start to *do* the things that your ideal self does. And that will set you well on your way to finally *having* what you want out of life.

Be. Do. Have.

CHAPTER 11

HABITS, RITUALS, AND THE FATAL FLAW OF NEW YEAR'S RESOLUTIONS

*"Excellence is an art won by training and habituation. . . .
We are what we repeatedly do. Excellence, then,
is not an act, but a habit."*

—ARISTOTLE

Making a resolution to become your ideal self is about as effective as making a resolution on New Year's Eve to lose weight.

It doesn't work.

Don't take that as a discouraging statement. Take it as an acknowledgment that making the same mistakes over and over again simply won't help you get where you want to go. If you want change to happen, you have to change.

Every New Year's Eve, nearly 60 percent of Americans make resolutions. These resolutions range greatly but usually center around key life areas like relationships, health, spirituality, and finances. Why do we make them? Because New Year's brings a moment of renewal, which gives us a feeling of inspiration. Inspiration tends to lead to clarity, and in an instant, we can articulate what we always knew: We need to make a change.

However, even though millions of people make resolutions each year, a study done by the University of Scranton showed that only 8 percent of those resolution makers achieve their resolutions.[1] Eight percent! Twenty-five percent of the resolution makers drop the resolutions within one week.[2]

These are promises that we make to ourselves to better our own lives. Why aren't more people able to follow through?

LIMITED WILLPOWER

Roy Baumeister, PhD, a professor at Florida State University, conducted groundbreaking research that I believe provides some direction. His research over two decades ago spurred dozens of follow-up studies that changed our view of self-discipline.[3]

In 1998, Dr. Baumeister invited students to his lab to try to solve a series of impossible geometry puzzles.[4] He wasn't expecting the students to solve them. That wasn't the point. What he wanted was to see how long they would last before they gave up.

Unbeknownst to the students, his research began before they even looked at the first puzzle. Before the test, they were kept in a waiting room that had a tray full of fresh-baked chocolate chip cookies. One group of students was allowed to eat the cookies, but the other was told to restrain themselves from even touching them. Instead, they could snack on some freshly cut radishes. Radishes! That group stared longingly at those cookies and had to physically restrain themselves from diving for the tray.

When it came time to take the test, the first group—the ones who were allowed to indulge—as well as a control group that wasn't subjected to any food temptations at all, lasted a good 20 minutes on the impossible test before giving up.

The other group? Those who had to use all sorts of self-discipline while being tempted by the sights and smells of cookies? That group gave up on the test after just 8 minutes.

What the experiment showed is that self-discipline is a finite resource. When it's expended in one area, it is weakened and depleted in other completely unrelated areas where self-discipline might also be needed. By using their self-discipline to not indulge in the cookies, these students didn't have as much self-discipline left to apply to the test.

THE MENTAL MUSCLE

Think of self-discipline (or willpower, grit, determination, hustle, whatever you want to call it) like a mental muscle. Just like any muscle in our bodies that can be exercised for only so long before it gives out, so too self-discipline can only be expended for a finite period before it weakens. That's why when you come home after a long day of work, it's so much harder to resist the bag of potato chips, control your temper, or stop endlessly watching YouTube videos. You used up your reservoir of self-control during the day and have very little left at night. Dr. Baumeister calls this state of depleted willpower "ego depletion" (*ego* in the Freudian sense of self, not arrogance).

The fact that we have a limited pool of self-discipline means that we can't just point ourselves in a new direction in a moment of inspiration and expect our minds and bodies to follow through to the end. That's why resolutions mostly fail. Once the initial novelty wears off—after the first few hours or days—our mental muscles weaken.

Our minds may have unlimited potential, but our self-discipline is limited. Everything we do that requires effort needs self-discipline. Even activities we love can stretch those mental muscles. Change requires doing things that are new, uncomfortable, and strenuous, and they deplete our willpower—and that's in addition to the other areas of life that continuously tax our minds.

To make a lasting change, we need to use our self-discipline with discretion. We need to allocate it strategically, so we don't use it all up and then fail.

THE DOWNSIDE OF NEUROPLASTICITY

Earlier in the book, we learned that neuroplasticity puts us in the driver's seat with our brains. However, with opportunity comes responsibility. The ability to create mental connections can be a resource for the good, but can have detrimental effects as well. Like creating a dirt path in the woods, the more times we walk in a specific direction, the more reinforced that path becomes. The problem is when that path leads us to the wrong place.

Ironically, some of our most stubborn habits and disorders are products of our plasticity. Once a particular routine becomes well established, it can prevent other, more beneficial changes from occurring.

This is why breaking a habit is so hard. Habits are just fixed ways of thinking. When you repeat the same actions, the neurological connections strengthen. Your brain picks up on certain cues that stimulate these connections, triggering the same responsive action. The cycle continues and strengthens itself each time until it feels automatic, almost effortless.

I'm not just talking about habits like biting your fingernails. I'm talking about habits like constantly doubting yourself, mismanaging your finances, not committing fully to a relationship, or reverting to the same destructive behaviors again and again. All of those things are habits that we fall into because of the neuroconnections that exist in our brains.

Habits are the products of solid mental connections. Breaking those connections require an enormous amount of mental effort and self-discipline.

So what do we need to do? How do we break our bad habits and replace them with new, healthier ones?

BEHAVIORS, NOT OUTCOMES

Resolutions are destined to fail because they are centered on an outcome. They articulate a destination, but don't give us a map showing us how to get there. There is no plan of action; only the expression of a desired effect.

With only the end in mind, you are not honing in on the specific behavior or belief that needs to be changed to actually get there. You can't prune out those negative neuroconnections that hold you back or chart a new course to achieve the goal.

Change is a process, not an outcome.

Resolutions are outcome focused.

Habits, on the other hand, are process focused.

Change happens when you form new habits, not new resolutions.

So how do we create new habits? Through rituals.

Rituals are designated routines, designed by us to bring change in a particular area of our lives. When repeated regularly, rituals target specific neurological conditioning and effectively create new neuroconnections, which lead us to new habits. The brain strengthens these neuroconnections, so that over time the new, desired action feels more automatic and effortless.

By allocating our limited self-discipline to a ritual, we are leveraging the power of neuroplasticity, as the brain will, over time, reduce the mental effort and self-discipline required to maintain the specific action. "Getting things down to routines and habits takes willpower at first," Baumeister said, "but in the long run conserves willpower."[5]

To clarify: A resolution is simply putting a name on the direction in which you want to go. To get there, you need to design rituals that will take you there. Along the way, the rituals become habits, triggering new neuroconnections, which prune away the bad habits and strengthen better ones, restructuring your brain for the better.[6]

By creating rituals aimed at getting you to your resolution, you won't just reach a resolution, you will live it. You will become it. It could take just 2 minutes a day, but if your rituals are consistent, then your brain will create new neuroconnections; over time, the action will feel more natural and effortless.

For example, think back to the ritual I mentioned earlier in the book: Start each day by writing down four things you are grateful for, which will lead you toward a resolution of being happier. At first, finding and writing down those four things may require extra self-discipline. But if you do it every day, your ritual will become a habit and, over time, will require less mental effort. Eventually, you get the benefits of recognizing things you're grateful for, which leads to being happier, without expending the same amount of self-discipline to maintain the action.

Real change isn't a matter of continuously forcing yourself to do something that you don't want to do or that feels unnatural. That may be an interim step you have to take—the idea of "fake it 'til you make it"—but that's not the goal. As we discussed earlier, friction between what you are doing and what you want to be doing will only lead you to give up. If you still have to force yourself, then you haven't changed. You are still the same person who, probably out of guilt, is trying to not be you.

If you want real change, you need to upgrade your neuroconnections. The way to do this is to harness the power of rituals.

LIKE BRUSHING YOUR TEETH

Do you remember brushing your teeth today?

Most people will pause, think back to their morning routines, and try to bring back the memory of brushing their teeth. In truth, they won't really remember it. They will have some vague recollection of brushing their teeth sometime recently, which could have actually been the day or week prior. They will look for something outside teeth brushing to jog their memories, maybe shaving or having a conversation or yelling at the person who kept knocking on the bathroom door.

When you first started brushing your teeth, it wasn't so easy. As a young child, you probably often forgot or deliberately avoided doing it. You wound up by the door waiting for the school bus when your mom yelled, "Did you brush your teeth?"

But as you got older, it became easier and easier because brushing your teeth is a great ritual. It's short, simple, and repeatable. It takes place at around the same time every day and every night, in the same room. It even connects to daily events: getting out of the shower in the morning or getting ready for bed at night.

And so, our minds form a mental connection for each aspect of the ritual, from taking the toothbrush to putting on the toothpaste to brushing our teeth, spitting, and rinsing. We repeat approximately the same action every day, and over time, the neuroconnections become so strong that it feels effortless to do it—so much so that we don't even remember doing it a few seconds after it's done. At that point, it has become a habit.[7]

That's the power of a ritual. If done well, it becomes a habit. It becomes so ingrained in our minds that it stops requiring the same amount of effort to do the action. As the effort required starts to diminish, you are left with the benefit of the ritual (clean teeth, a healthy mouth) and can allocate that mental effort elsewhere (picking out clothes, washing the dishes, eating dinner). That's the essential reason why rituals and habits are so powerful: Over time, they require less conscious intention and self-discipline. And when they're focused in a positive manner, they yield long-term, incredibly positive benefits.

Nobel laureate, psychologist, and bestselling author Daniel Kahneman sheds additional insight on the power of rituals in his book *Thinking, Fast and Slow*. The mind processes information in two distinct ways: "System 1," the brain's fast, automatic, intuitive approach; and "System 2," the mind's slower, analytical mode. System 1 is the more powerful of the systems and typically dictates System 2. Rituals are the way to put System 2 (our thoughtful mind) back in control by training System 1 to take over the tasks that System 2 is doing, freeing up cognitive capacity in System 2 while benefitting from the results of the new habit.[8]

As Dr. William James, the famous psychologist, once said: "[O]nly when habits of order are formed can we advance to really interesting fields of action."[9]

BE A WORLD-CLASS PERFORMER

Stephen King is one of the most prolific writers of our time. Over the course of his career, he has written 55 novels, hundreds of short stories, and half a dozen nonfiction books.

How? He has a ritual. Every day, he writes 10 pages.[10]

When you write 10 pages a day, you are habituating writing in your brain. It requires less effort each time. Your mind is freed up to have more creative thoughts, which you can more easily articulate.

King didn't become a prolific writer because of a resolution; it was because of his rituals. He may have had a resolution, but it wasn't the resolution that got him to the finish line. It was his rituals, which became his habits.

Take a moment to think of other world-class individuals you admire—musicians, athletes, entrepreneurs. Go online or pick up one of their biographies, and read about the rituals they use to get things done. Chances are, anyone you can think of who has achieved world-class status follows a strict schedule of rituals. Their days are structured and repeated. Is that a coincidence? No! Those rituals are what led them to success. Establishing positive rituals are what will lead you to success in your own life, too.

Leo Tolstoy, famed author of *War and Peace*, never missed a day of writing. In his diary, he explained, "I must write each day without fail, not so much for the success of the work, as in order not to get out of my routine."[11]

Benjamin Franklin would get up every day at 5 a.m. and follow a strict schedule of introspection, work, and even fun. Every morning, he would ask himself, "What good shall I do this day?" Between 5 and 7 a.m., he would wash, "contrive day's business, and take the resolution of the day; prosecute the present study, and breakfast." Between 8 and 11 a.m., he would work. At noon, he would read, look over his accounts, and "dine." In the afternoon, again he would work, then in the evening, he would ask, "What good have I done this day?" The hours between 6 and 9 p.m. were spent cleaning, putting things in their place, eating supper, and engaging in "diversions" such as music. The remaining hours? "Sleep."[12]

What we learn from some of history's most successful individuals is that rituals are the path to incredible results.

INTEGRATING WHAT YOU KNOW

Now it's time to put your knowledge into action. It's time to *do*. Before any transformation can occur, action is required. *Be. Do. Have.*

A good way to look at this is to look back at how you learned to drive a car.

First, you decided to be a driver. You signed up for driver's ed. You learned the rules in the book. You got your permit. You gained a basic understanding of driving and started to see things differently, noticing red lights, stop signs, and directional signs you may have never noticed before. But you still didn't know how to drive.

Next, you got behind the wheel and practiced. The first few times, you went real slow and maybe bumped into a few things. You may have even done something really bad or embarrassing and thought you would never get the hang of it. But as discouraging as it was, you never once considered giving up completely. You knew that these growing pains were an unfortunate but inevitable part of the process.

Then, practicing driving on a regular basis changed you. You repeated the same actions again and again. As you kept practicing, the knowledge went from conscious to subconscious (or as Kahneman would say, from System 2 to System 1). The knowledge integrated into practical life and transformed your ability to drive!

Now, you're a driver. You can always drive. Period. You will never go back to not being a driver. If you don't drive for a year or even 10 years, you can pick it up again in a fraction of the time. You can get behind the wheel of a vehicle you've never driven before and figure out pretty quickly how to start it and put it in gear and go wherever you need to go. You adapt to driving new vehicles with relative ease. There are even times when you drive without thinking about it. You're going along, listening to the radio, and you realize you don't even remember the last 5 miles. Yet you don't crash. Why? Because driving is automatic. It's a part of you. *You* now includes being a driver.

This same process works with good and bad habits, so it's important to pay attention to what you're doing and not doing on a daily basis. Look at it. Learn from it. Know there will be setbacks that you will overcome.

Here is the process again, so you can visualize it.

1. Be: Deciding what you want to *be* opens us up to new beliefs, upgrading our mental schema and seeing new possibilities. This can be uncomfortable since your mind doesn't have any neuroconnections that feel familiar. That will change as you start to *do*.

2. Do: Taking action forces you to integrate knowledge into your mind, since engaging your body requires your brain to create a plethora of new neuroconnections.[13] Allocating your limited willpower to specific repeatable actions increases the likelihood that you will be able to do them consistently, creating new habits.

3. Have: The repetition reinforces the behavior, which strengthens these new connections, effectively changing your mind and leaving the new behaviors feeling "natural." You haven't just achieved your goal, you are living it.

ELEMENTS OF A RITUAL

How do you create rituals that will work? What are the elements of an effective ritual?

Element 1: Distinguish "You" from Your Habits

As we discussed in the previous chapter, identity is an important aspect of your schema. How you see yourself forms a baseline for how you assess your actions.

It is all too easy to identify yourself with the habits that are holding you back. "I'm bad with money." "I can't keep a relationship longer than 6 months." "I never liked working out." All of these statements reflect neuroconnections that prevent us from living the life we want. They feel like you since you are habituated to do them. However, your neuroconnections are not you. Your neuroconnections are like muscles, like your abs. You are not your abs; you have abs. You are not your mind; you have a mind. You are more than your mental structure, and you are capable of changing it at any time.

If you want to change a habit, you have to make sure to not identify with it. You don't act destructively; you have just been habituated to act destructively.

Now, this is not to say that disassociating with your habits shifts the burden of responsibility. On some level, you are ultimately responsible for letting those bad habits continue. But acknowledging the fact that they are fundamentally separate from you accomplishes something positive: It enables you to attack those bad habits and get rid of them, the way a healthy body repels a virus.

Remember: The traits that define your life today do not have to define your life tomorrow. All you have to do is replace them with rituals that habituate you toward a greater destination.

Element 2: Make It Ambitious and Exciting

If you are going to change, you have to make a deliberate choice. It can't be based on the nagging of your doctor, spouse, or children. It can't be based on guilt or regret. The choice needs to be made by you, for you. It needs to align with your inner needs. It needs to be something about which you get excited and see yourself accomplishing.

Focus on your ideal self, and push yourself to articulate a vision that inspires you and empowers you to try to achieve that vision.

Inspiration lasts when it comes from within. There are only so many times a song, a book, or conversation with a loved one will inspire you to keep going or growing. True inspiration is self-generated. It happens when you see who you could be. You feel the possibility of becoming someone you dream of. That inner feeling is the core of your inspiration. External inspiration only reinforces that inner feeling.

Dr. Daniel Goleman explains why it's so important for you to be inspired about your vision: "Changing habits is hard work. One need only to think back to one's success and failures with New Year's resolutions to find ample evidence of this. Whenever people try to change habits of how they think and act, they must reverse . . . highly reinforced neural circuitry, built up over years of repeating the habit. That's why lasting change requires a strong commitment to a future vision of oneself."[14]

Once you can express what you want deep down, that image of yourself becomes inspiring. You can feel it. You can see it, and now you know what direction to go. When it's ambitious and exciting, you are going to want to get it.

Element 3: Go from "All or Nothing" to "+1"

While your new vision has to be ambitious and exciting, your rituals must be within your reach. Taking on a ritual that you cannot sustain is like making a resolution; it will ultimately lead you to get frustrated and dejected. The key is consistency. Better to do less and keep it up than overreach and end up back where you started, or worse.

If you want to effect real change, you need to adapt to how

your brain works. The best way is to identify a ritual that is just outside of your grasp. I call it a "+1 Action." Look at your daily routine and ask yourself what would be an action that is just outside of your normal behavior, an action that requires you to stretch but not be in too much pain. A "+1 Action" will start you on your journey to your goal, without adding too much stress to your life. This way, you will be able to use your limited self-discipline to see it through.[15]

For example, if you are looking to lose weight, going to the gym may be the linchpin to all the other aspects of weight loss. Once at the gym, you are most likely going to exercise. In crafting a ritual, I wouldn't advise doing a full workout routine. The ritual can be, "Just go to the gym." Don't set any goal beyond getting in the door if that's all you can handle. Heck, walk in and walk out! Just make sure you do it every day. That may be enough to start the larger cascade of benefits. Then add one workout—just the bike or the bench press or something—and do that one thing until you're ready for more.

Find a ritual that is one level beyond where you are. Something reasonable, doable, and nonthreatening. Then do it. Consistently. No matter what.

Element 4: Make It Clear, Simple, and Measurable

Once you choose your ritual, you need to clarify all of the actions involved. What are you actually doing? When? For how long? What do you consider success? Failure?

The clearer the ritual is and the simpler each action is, the easier it is to measure it. And measuring your progress is critical if you want to gauge its impact. If you track your progress, you will be able to add another ritual if you are doing great, or readjust if you are failing.

Jerry Seinfeld, one of the most famous comedians in the world, has spoken about how he prints out a big full-year calendar and hangs it on his wall. He makes a habit of writing new material every single day. That's how he stays fresh and comes up with new jokes. It's a ritual that has become a habit. And he tracks that habit. Every day that he writes, even a little bit, he marks an X on the calendar.[16] He makes sure that the chain of Xs never ends.

This ritual played a huge part in landing him a career that boasts one of the most successful TV shows of all time, one of the most lucrative TV syndication deals of all time, and the financial freedom to do everything and anything he wants. He's raising kids with his wife and collecting Porsches in his apartment building–size garage in New York City. He's touring the world doing stand-up shows in front of adoring audiences, and he recently created a web series, *Comedians in Cars Getting Coffee*, that connected him to two things he loves: fellow comedians and classic cars. He apparently did that series for his own amusement, but it's become a bona fide hit that has brought even more success into his life. It's fascinating how following your passions and acting as your ideal self can do that.

With all the complexity of his life, Seinfeld's ritual is clear, simple, and measurable. That's why he has been willing to sustain it from year to year. And he never gave it up. Even after the success came.

So how do you go about choosing the right rituals for your life and your goals, rituals that will work for and support your ideal self?

TAKING THE STEPS

In the last chapter, we explored the idea of writing out your ideal day and trying to tease from that what it is you want to Be.

Let's start there, with that document. The ideal day is filled with what you are doing. From there, you should have developed a list of things you want to *be*.

So now, how do you make it happen?

Ask yourself: For each thing that I want to be, what does that person do? What does a great parent do? What does a successful entrepreneur do? What does a healthy person do? What does a generous person do?

As you think about what those people do, be specific. What time do they get up? How much time do they spend reading? Honing their skills? Learning about their competition? What do they eat for breakfast? Do they snack? How much time do they put into working out? Being at home? Being totally present in conversations?

From there, try to gauge how you compare and then create a ritual that you can do on a regular basis to get yourself closer to your ideal self. For example, if I believe that successful people read every day, I might make a ritual of reading every day. I may not be able to read for an hour, and I may not finish a book every week, but I am going to set aside at least 10 minutes every day and never miss it.

If I know the best entrepreneurs get up early to plan their day, I'm going to set my vision to get up earlier every day. I may not be able to get up at 5:00 a.m., but I can get up 20 minutes earlier than I usually do to give myself a little more time to prepare for my day.

If I know that in order to grow my relationships I need to spend quality time with my family, and yet I'm always on my phone when I'm home, then I need to establish a new ritual. Every night when I get home, I'm going to put my phone away for 30 minutes.

The idea is to start with one thing. Create a ritual, a clear action you're going to do on a regular basis that is connected to your larger vision, something one step past where you are right now. Be honest with yourself about what you can handle and discipline yourself to keep moving up one step at a time. One foot in front of the next. That's the balance of great vision and great rituals. Vision and action. Clouds and rocks. Plan in the spiritual, implement in the physical. That's how true growth works.

To build muscle, you lift a certain amount of weight, and after a while you increase your weight. It's the same for running: You start with a certain distance, then you add more and more distance. Our lives are more complex than running a marathon or lifting weights. But a good ritual gets around the complexity. A ritual is simple and is something you can do every day, with no days off. (Okay, one day off. You need recovery time.) If you can do the ritual every day, you will wake up in the not-too-distant future and realize you've become that new person you wanted to be.

Continuing the exercise we worked on in Chapter 10, go ahead and add one more column: the ritual that will move you toward your *be*.

EXERCISE IV: ESTABLISHING RITUALS

VISION	BE	RITUAL (DO)	FREQUENCY
Get in shape	Healthy	Exercise every day	6 days a week
Lose weight	Healthy	Replace soda with water	7 days a week
My wife feels fully valued and loved	A great husband	Communicate appreciation to her by putting my cell phone away and talking to her for 30 minutes when I get home from work	5 days a week
Grow in my career; get that big promotion	Successful	Read industry-related material	5 days a week

For a downloadable copy of this chart, go to charlieharary.com/book.

Your vision is who you want to *be*, and your action is what you *do* about it. Unless your vision is big and inspires you, you're never going to do anything. But if you can be inspired to strive for a greater life, and if you can be patient enough to put small repeatable actions into practice, then every single step on the road will be encouraging—not because you feel guilty, worried, or bad, but because each step connects to a long, exciting journey, one you visualized and one that taps into your ideal self.

Don't try to do everything all at once. You've tried that before, and it doesn't work. Instead, add one ritual. Then, once it's more habituated, once it's mentally easier, once you do it without expending loads of self-discipline, either make that ritual more challenging or create a new ritual in another area of your life.

Gauge yourself. If you find that you're taking two or three days off in a row, that ritual isn't working for you. Step back. Make it smaller. Stick with it.

Most of all, stay excited! This is you improving. You have the ability to change your neuroprogramming, to change your schemas, to dig down to who you really are and inch closer and closer to who you want to be.

Remember, today's habits will determine tomorrow's success.

Big vision. Small steps.

CHAPTER 12

THE CROSSOVER: FINDING FLOW IN AN OVERSTIMULATED WORLD

"I have known a great many troubles, but most of them never happened."

—MARK TWAIN

H e is going to be just fine," the doctor said to the packed waiting room of anxious faces.

After the long hours, many tears, and hundreds of cell phone minutes, the doctor's report that the operation was successful let all of us breathe a huge sigh of relief.

That was how my night ended one Thursday five years ago. It started with my friend at a Knicks game. Midway through the game, he received a frantic call that his dad had collapsed. We raced to the hospital to find that his dad had suffered a sudden heart attack and was already in the operating room for emergency surgery.

My friend's father was discharged soon after. He recovered for a short period at home and went right back to normal life.

A few months later, I asked my friend how his father was doing.

"Honestly," he said, "he's a changed man."

"Really?" I probed. "How?"

He answered, "My father told me that as he was being wheeled into the operating room, the only thoughts in his mind were all the things that he had wanted to do but didn't. The calls he didn't make, the conversations he didn't have, the activities he didn't do."

My friend paused as if to reflect and then continued, "He didn't want to quit his job or change his life. He loves my mom, he loves us, he loves his work. . . . He just thought he'd have more time. He had no advance warning that his life may be over without having done those things. When he recovered, he made a conscious decision to live his life with three letters."

"Three letters?" I asked.

"Yes," he responded. "N. O. W. He wrote those letters on his business card and put it on his mirror. Each morning, he sees it, and it reminds him to not wait for tomorrow or next month. He talks, acts, and works with a sense of purpose that he never had before."

He paused again. "It's amazing," he said. "The doctors saved his life, but those three letters *changed* his life."

THE VALUE OF BEING PRESENT

We've all heard stories like this before, haven't we? We've certainly heard the mantras: "Be present." "Live in the now." "Live like there's no tomorrow." "What if today was your last day."

What my friend's dad explained about the impact of N.O.W. is that in everything he would do from that moment forward, he would *be there, now.* "When I talk to your mother, I am there, now. I'm not distracted," his dad told him. "During the conversation, I am not thinking about tomorrow's schedule. When I eat, I enjoy the meal *now.* I'm not scarfing it down so I can keep on racing through my day. In everything I do, I'm fully invested in that moment."

What my friend's father discovered is perhaps one of the most important keys to unlocking greatness in our lives.

When we talk about taking on new rituals, we need to remember that rituals are routines designed to change our minds. We want to create and reinforce new neurological connections. If we are not fully engaged in the actions we are doing, those actions will not have the mental impact we desire.

So as we move from the vision of the ideal to the implementation of the ritual, we need to ensure that in everything we do, we are there. Fully engaged. Not distracted or preoccupied. We have to live the three letters: N.O.W.

Why? Because being fully present is the path to finding our flow.

FINDING FLOW

Mihaly Csikszentmihalyi was a young kid from Budapest, Hungary, whose family escaped just as the Nazis were increasing their grip on Eastern Europe. At the age of 22, Mihaly wound up in the United States with no money and no English skills (other than what he'd picked up in some comic books). He managed to get into the University of Illinois and ultimately the psychology department at the University of Chicago, where he earned tenure less than a decade later.

Since that time, his life has been dedicated to understanding why we do what we do and how we can put ourselves in an optimal state of performance. In his work, Csikszentmihalyi introduced a key distinction between two types of experiences: those that are autotelic and those that are exotelic.[1]

Auto is from the Greek word *auto*, which means "self." *Telic* is "goal" or "purpose" from the Greek word *telos*, which means "end." When one engages in an activity for its intrinsic purpose, for the sake of the activity itself, it's called an autotelic experience. If you're engaging in an activity for some external reward, it's an exotelic experience (*exo* means "outside" or "external").

For example, when you come home from work and see your children playing ball outside, they are engaged in an autotelic experience. There is no external reason for playing. They are not doing it for an athletic scholarship or increased popularity. They are playing because they are having fun, and the game itself is the reward. However, when you scream out the window, "Time for homework!" they transition to having an exotelic experience. They don't want to do homework. So we have to convince them that if they don't understand fifth-grade math, then they won't get into high school or college, they won't find jobs, and their whole lives will collapse. They reluctantly agree but don't enjoy it. They are doing it for an external reason.

Csikszentmihalyi wanted to find out the impact of these distinct experiences. How does an autotelic experience feel? Does it impact performance? Do people really ever excel at exotelic experiences, even when the rewards are great? Or are people always more motivated when engaging in autotelic experiences?

He gave people pagers (this was back before smartphones existed). He paged them at random times throughout their days and asked them to jot down information about what they were doing and how it felt. He tracked all of this information and compiled it, and he discovered that when people were engaged in autotelic experiences—meaning they were doing something for its intrinsic sake—they felt different.[2]

It was from this research that he uncovered the concept of "flow."

When we engage in an activity that's autotelic, for its own sake, we enter into a state of mind in which we're connected to the experience at a much deeper level. We feel differently when we're in this state. Life is at its fullest, and it's almost as if time stops. We don't need to eat. We are, as he says, in flow: a state of concentration or complete absorption with the activity at hand.

The Flow is an optimal state of performance, where the person is fully immersed in what he is doing. It's a feeling everyone has had at times—on the pitcher's mound striking out batter after batter; "leveling up" in *Call of Duty*; soloing on a guitar and feeling deeply connected to the music; typing a paper due in the morning as the words are flying from your fingertips.

It seems obvious that we should try to engage in as many autotelic experiences as we can, because it's in those experiences that we become our best. It's in those moments when we enjoy our lives the most, because life feels justified in the present, instead of being held hostage to some future gain.

An exotelic experience is when the activity you engage in is for an external reason. This reason could be mundane, like for money or an award, or something loftier, like supporting your family or helping people. The challenge with exotelic experiences is that while you're engaged in them, you feel as if you're wasting your time, since you are only doing them for the eventual benefit. You wish you could just hurry up and get to the benefit. So the activity itself feels meaningless.

Most people view their jobs as exotelic, which is why they are so unhappy at the office. They feel that their invested mental energy does nothing to strengthen their sense of self. Since they are generally unhappy at work, they need an escape, so they search for leisure time. Leisure generally consists of passively absorbing information, without using any skills or exploring new opportunities for action, which after a short while is boring. As a result, life passes as a sequence of anxious and boring experiences over which a person has little control.

You may be thinking. "Who wouldn't love to do what they enjoy? But I have responsibilities." Most people can't just quit their jobs or run around the world. Most people spend large portions of their lives on what they have to do, not what they want to do.

Here is where Csikszentmihalyi's research gets even more interesting.

What he found was that flow doesn't only have to occur when you are engaged in what you want to be doing. It's a state of mind that we can bring into every endeavor. When you become fully engaged in something, the *engagement* itself will make that activity more enjoyable.

Exotelic experiences, Csikszentmihalyi discovered, can be *converted* into autotelic ones. That means almost everything you do, even the tasks you dislike, can be made more autotelic.

Look at your life right now and identify tasks that are exotelic. Maybe it's chores around the house or an organizational task at work. What flow research shows us is that if you focus yourself on being fully engaged in that activity, fully present, not only will you do it better (and quicker), but you'll also enjoy it more.

Now, you don't want to spend your entire life doing things that don't lead you to your ideal self, but by leveraging the power of being present, you can be more successful and happier at anything you are doing.

What flow teaches us is that being present isn't just a nice idea that you hear in self-help books. Being present is a scientifically backed strategy for success.

So how can we implement this if life is just too busy? If we are juggling responsibilities all day? How can we find the time to be present when we feel pulled in every direction?

THE CROSSOVER

Years ago, I was flying to Texas and wound up sitting next to an NCAA basketball coach. It was a dream come true for me. I don't think he realized how little sleep he was going to get on that flight once he introduced himself. Having played varsity basketball in high school, I started quizzing him on everything I could think of, remembering back to my games and asking about plays, presses, defenses, and picks. We were only a half hour into this conversation when he ordered some alcohol. It was going to be a long flight for him.

At one point, I asked him, "What's the hardest move in basketball?"

"Oh, that's easy," he said.

"The fadeaway?" I asked.

"Nope."

"The pick-and-roll?" I asked.

"Nope," he said. "The crossover. Very few players can master the crossover. It's the hardest move because you've got to get the defender to actually believe what you're doing. Most people just kind of fake it a little bit, and it doesn't really work. The greatest players in the game—Michael Jordan, Kobe Bryant, Allen Iverson—these guys made their careers on mastering that crossover."

"Well, what's the secret to a great crossover?" I asked him.

He smiled, as if I were one of his players. "You have to be able to go all-in in one direction and then, on a dime, turn and go all-in in the other direction. If you're not all-in, the defender won't get faked out—so when you switch and go the other way, he'll be there with you. You can't just fake it. You have to actually go in that direction and then switch as soon as he bites."

I have often thought about how important the crossover is, not just in a basketball game, but in life. In the modern world, we have become the consummate multitaskers, being pulled in a hundred directions at once and operating in multiple environments at the same time. We wake up in the morning, and we're partly on our phones and partly on our e-mails and partly with our families and partly watching TV and partly at work and partly thinking of the future, while partly thinking of the past.

If you remember from earlier in the book, our nervous systems can only process about 110 bits of information per second. Allocate that across hundreds of different tasks, and we wind up an inch deep and a mile wide. That's why we're never really great at anything. We're never really *in* anything.

The University of London did research on what happens to the brain when we multitask. The study found that in people who multitask during cognitive tasks, IQ levels are significantly reduced—to the same degree that IQ is reduced by smoking marijuana or staying up all night.[3] Some men in the study saw their IQ levels reduced to that of an 8-year-old. (Women didn't see as significant a decline, which inadvertently proved the adage that women are better multitaskers than men. But the point is that both men and women saw significant declines in IQ.)[4]

Another study at the University of Sussex looked at the MRI scans of the brains of people who spent time on multiple devices. What they found is that frequent multitaskers actually had less brain density in the anterior cingulate cortex—a region responsible for empathy as well as cognitive and emotional control.[5]

That can't be good.

All of this leads to a cascading problem for us: Doing something without being fully present decreases the enjoyment you have for the activity and the likelihood that the action will be fully effective. So we are less successful and less happy, which makes us more distracted and less present. And the downward spiral continues.

As Roman philosopher Publilius Syrus put it, "To do two things at once is to do neither."[6]

ALL IN

I remember the time I was throwing a football around in the backyard with my son, and at one point he looked at me and said, "Daddy, are you okay?"

"Yeah, I'm okay. Why?"

"Because you keep throwing it over my head!"

And I realized: I wasn't okay. We were having a catch, but only around 10 percent of me was mentally present. I was 50 percent worrying about something that happened that day at work, 20 percent thinking about the next day, 10 percent wondering if the phone in my pants pocket had just buzzed, and 10 percent thinking to myself, "When is this going to be over? We've already thrown the ball back and forth 30 times, and we need to get back inside."

If you would have told me 20 years earlier, "One day, you are going to get to have a catch with your child in the backyard," I'd have said, "That's my greatest dream!" And here I was, tossing a football around in my backyard, and I wasn't *there*.

How many moments like that had I missed? How many experiences had I completely let slip by because my mind was in so many different places at once that I was actually nowhere?

In her bestselling book, *All Joy and No Fun*, Jennifer Senior provides an insight into why studies on working moms found lower levels of happiness than nonparents, and little satisfaction in parenting in general. It was the same reason why I wasn't enjoying playing ball with my kid: When they were with their kids, they weren't *with* their kids. They were constantly multitasking. They weren't present. Working moms were so busy that even though they loved their children, their experiences with them were not pleasurable because they constantly felt rushed and distracted.[7] When they're at work, they feel guilty for not being with the family; and when they're with the family, they feel guilty for not being at work. Always feeling like there's somewhere else you should be is draining and unenjoyable.

What the research suggested was that if these moms—the same goes for dads—could just be present with their kids, they would enjoy those experiences more. Being present means that you feel that you're in the right place at the right time. And when you allow yourself that feeling at home, you not only enjoy being at home, but you are more effective and then don't carry the same guilt with you into the office (and vice versa).

You can't be your best—and you can't feel your best—at anything, unless you're fully focused on it. Only once you're *all-in* can you convert exotelic experiences into autotelic ones.

This feels a little unrealistic, doesn't it? Parents aren't trying to be distracted from their children, they are just trying to balance everything. Many people feel like they are pulled in a million directions because of their daily responsibilities. Between a mortgage, carpool, Little League, work, traffic . . . it's hard to manage everything. And on top of all that, we carry around a device that buzzes all day with more and more stimuli that clamors for our attention.

We're all juggling too many balls, and we feel like we can't let any of them drop. How are we supposed to find time to be fully present in anything?

Therein lies the power of the crossover.

THE PIVOT

The crossover is the hardest move in basketball because it requires going all-in in one direction and then, in a moment, going all-in a different way. Each direction is quarantined. The skill is in the pivot. If you could see into the mind of a player during the move, you would see how confident he is in choosing one direction, knowing he has the ability to switch, or cross over, at just the right moment.

Most of us can't be fully present for long periods of time. There is too much going on. We can't get lost in a book or a sculpture or any project for hours on end. However, we can be present for 15 minutes at a time. We can be present for a half hour.

That's where the magic happens. If we learn to pivot, to cross over to the matters that clamor for our attention, we will allow ourselves to be fully present in each of those moments throughout our day. How does that look? For the 20 minutes you work on a project, you're all-in. Then you get home, and for the time you spend with your kids, you're all-in. Then you pivot and spend time with your spouse, and you're all-in. Then you pivot and check your e-mails, and you're all-in.

The essence of the crossover is that you get to go all-in for brief moments of your day. That will give you the benefits of being present, while still maintaining balance in your life.

THE DAILY TIME ALLOCATION

So how do we do it? How do we perfect the crossover?

We know from Dr. Baumeister's chocolate chip cookie study (in Chapter 11) that willpower is finite and resolutions don't last. Deciding, or resolving, to be more present in your life won't make you more present. What we need to do is go back to the last chapter, to our rituals, and use them to help us practice going all-in.

Let's add another column to the chart we've been working on. Take a look at your rituals and ask yourself how long it will take to properly complete the identified rituals. Decide that just for those particular minutes, you're going to be all-in. That's the time you allocated for the ritual, and all you are going to focus on during that allocation is that ritual.

For the 20 minutes jogging, the 5 minutes calling your spouse, the 15 minutes reading, whatever it is, go all-in on those rituals. Focus on them with your whole heart and mind. Don't let anything else get in the way, either externally or in your mind. Silence your phone, don't check e-mail—remove the triggers that typically distract you. Give yourself both permission and a mandate to be completely *in* those rituals, and keep doing it until it feels natural.

EXERCISE V: GOING ALL-IN

BE	VISION	RITUAL (DO)	FREQUENCY	DAILY TIME ALLOCATION
Fit	Get in shape	Exercise	6 days a week	20–60 minutes
Healthy	Lose weight	Replace soda with water	7 days a week	2 minutes
A great husband	My wife feels fully valued and loved	Communicate appreciation to her by putting my cell phone away and talking to her for 30 minutes when I get home from work	5 days a week	30 minutes
Successful	Grow in my career; get that big promotion	Read industry-related material	5 days a week	20 minutes

For a downloadable copy of this chart, go to charlieharary.com/book.

Doing this will accomplish two things: First, going all-in will make those rituals much richer and stronger, which will increase your neuroconnections and make your rituals more effective. Second, the practice of being present will be reinforced in your mind. By going all-in on your rituals, you'll be creating neuroconnections about how to go all-in on everything. You get twice the bang for your buck. You're habituating not only the ritual but also your capacity to be present!

As you do that, you will leverage the power of your mind to gain more control of your life. You'll see just how much enjoyment can be found in the tasks at hand. You'll be more engaged in what you do and become better at it. You'll be happier and more effective, enabling you to better achieve success.

And once you do that, you'll be well on your way to where you want to go.

CHAPTER 13

THE ROAD TRIP: UTILIZING YOUR GOLDEN LEVER

"I wish I'd had the courage to live a life true to myself and not the life others expected of me."

—A COMMON REGRET FROM PEOPLE ON THEIR DEATHBEDS, AS TOLD BY NURSE BRONNIE WARE[1]

A few years ago, I took my family on a road trip for vacation. We planned to drive down the East Coast from our home in New York. We packed the kids in the minivan and had a whole itinerary planned with sightseeing, restaurants, and rest stops, culminating in a two-day stay at a hotel in North Carolina.

No sooner had we pulled out of our driveway and turned the corner when my 4-year-old said, "Daddy? Are we there yet?"

"Ummm, no, honey. We just left the driveway," I said.

"Okay, thanks," he responded, looking out the window.

Five minutes later, we were still in my neighborhood, stopped at a red light, and he spoke up again: "Are we there yet?"

"No," I told him. "We're not even close."

Twenty minutes later, he asked the question again. This time, I started to get a little hot under the collar. I tried to explain that it was going to be a very long trip and that I'd tell him when we were there—at which point, he did what every 4-year-old does when he isn't getting his way: He crossed his arms and said, "It's not fair. I want to be at the hotel now!"

As we drove, I thought, "What a shame. He's missing the point. It's a road trip." Part of the fun is the road. It's enjoying the experiences along the way.

That's how life works, too. As products of an educational system that seems to constantly prepare us for the next stage, we're trained to think that life is about getting to the next level. You want to get to high school quicker. You want to skip right through college. You want to get out into the working world. You want to be an executive younger. You want to be *there* already. The idea that there is some end that you're going toward means there is a destination to strive for. So we constantly ask ourselves: Am I there yet? I'm 25, am I there yet? I'm 40, am I there yet? I'm 60, am I there yet?

We've developed a destination-focused mind-set. This schema has caused us an incredible amount of pain and frustration. We keep looking around to see where everybody else is, trying to figure out if we're ahead or behind them—even as they themselves are asking, "Am I there yet?"

By focusing solely on the destination, we miss most of the experiences along the way. We miss out on the best parts of life, which usually take place on the road to where we're going. We don't value those moments that seem to deviate us from reaching a prize that always seems to dissolve in our hands.

That's the problem. The end is never actually there. As you get to the finish line, you realize that they've moved the ribbon. So you keep running, until you wake up one morning and realize that there is no finish line. There never was. There is no end, no destination to get to.

Life is not about the destination. Life is about the journey. The people who recognize this understand that when you go all-in on every step of the journey, you get the most out of life.

Researchers have seen this again and again. In his famous TED Talk, "The Surprising Science of Happiness," Daniel Gilbert, PhD, professor at Harvard's school of psychology, noted that attaining goals doesn't lead to happiness. When you attain a goal, he explained, you may get a spike in happiness, but usually you go right back to the baseline of where you were before that goal was achieved.[2]

THE PURPOSE OF GOALS

Life is not about achieving your goals; it's about *having* goals to achieve.

Let me explain.

Having goals is what liberates you in the present moment. It gives you a place to go, a direction, a path, a compass. And only when you have somewhere to go can you enjoy the ride.

Have you ever driven to a new place without a clear sense of where you're going? It felt like it took forever, right? But then on the way home, the same drive felt much shorter. Why? Because you knew where you were going. And as soon as you know where you're going, you get to enjoy the ride.

However, goals aren't meant to be destinations. Goals are meant to set a direction in which to head. It is the ride itself that is most important, not the destination.

In their extensive studies of happiness, psychology professors David Myers, PhD, of Hope College, and Ed Diener, PhD, of the

University of Illinois, confirmed that when it comes to happiness, the purpose of a goal is not to achieve it; rather, it's a direction that we are supposed to grow toward.[3]

Goals are the proverbial carrots in front of the racing rabbits. Setting the right goals and focusing on the path to achieve them create a platform, an opportunity, for self-growth and improvement. Attaining a desired goal is not as crucial as the journey you will take in doing so. We grow through the process of reaching our goals and then setting new goals that move us further in the direction we want to go.

But how do we know we're setting goals that move us in the right direction? That goes back to defining your ideal self. That is your ultimate goal, your *be,* for whom you set rituals and develop new habits to support.

But once you're on the journey, it's all about leaving your comfort zone.

GETTING RIPPED

I'll never forget the first time I asked a trainer to assist me at the gym. I had been going to the gym for months but was hardly seeing any results. I couldn't understand why.

"So," he started. "Show me what you do."

I went through my routine, using each machine and smiling each time with pride. I expected him to be impressed, but when I looked over at him I could see he was literally holding back laughter.

"Sorry," he said apologetically. "Of course you're not seeing results. You're not even working out."

"What do you mean?" I asked. "I'm here every day for an hour and a half, five days a week! I do every machine!"

"Doing the machines doesn't matter," he said. "If you're always doing the same amount of weight, you're not working your muscles. You're just going through the motions."

"Really?" I said.

"If you want to see results, follow this rule: When you're lifting weights, the last three of your set of repetitions have to *kill*. They really have to hurt. If they don't kill, your muscles don't grow."

"Why?" I asked. (I ask that a lot.)

"For your muscles to grow, the microfibers in your muscles have to tear. When you lift weights, you have to lift enough to tear those fibers. Then, with the proper rest and protein, your muscles rebuild themselves to get stronger and larger. After that, you lift even heavier weights, and the process repeats itself."

"Okay," I said. I was sure he had oversimplified the muscle-building process, but at least it made some sense to me. "So, what is the correct weight to lift?"

"There is no correct weight," he answered. "It depends on the person. The only thing you need to worry about is whether the weight is heavy enough to make the last three reps kill. You can't look to someone else to determine how much to lift. It's only about your muscles. You can't fool your body. You have to push your muscles to failure so they rebuild stronger."

I started following his advice, making the last three *kill*, and I saw more results in 6 weeks than I'd seen in the previous 6 months.

To me, that became the ultimate metaphor for finding success in life.

THE TWO TYPES OF SUCCESS

There are two types of success: horizontal and vertical. Each day, we stand at the crossroads of both, and our actions, thoughts, and feelings take us down one road or the other.

Horizontal success is entirely based on others. It's when you look "horizontally" and measure yourself relative to those around you. Your yardstick of success is how you compare to everyone else.

As we mentioned earlier in the book, in so many areas of life—from our careers to our personal relationships—we measure success in horizontal terms. When we live our lives constantly comparing ourselves to others, we will never achieve true success because we are not lifting the right weights. We are not doing the right rituals. Our *doing* is not sourced from our *being*. We approach life by looking around to see what others are doing. We are not cultivating our own talents and skills. We are not using our challenges to grow stronger. We are not lifting the weights that develop our muscles. And in the same way that you can't fool your body into building your muscles, you can't fool your soul into feeling fulfilled.

Don't get me wrong—we can all strive to get into good schools, enjoy fulfilling careers, and have enough money to buy what we want. But we should not make the mistake of thinking that having more than someone else equals true success.

What is true success? Vertical success.

Vertical success is when we stop looking around and start looking inside to see how we can grow. Vertical success is when we take whatever has been given to us—our strengths and our weaknesses, our background and current circumstances—and invest the effort into unlocking our potential for greatness. Our only yardstick is that potential. We look for ways to push ourselves to make today the best it can be. We stop comparing ourselves to others, how someone else is doing and what they are up to in life; we stop paying attention to others' opinions and what they think of us.

Vertical success is about constantly leaving our comfort zone and looking for ways to slowly rip the microfibers of our being, every day, knowing that even if we don't have the strength today, ripping makes us stronger tomorrow.[4] The aim of this is not to win some prize. It's to win the life you crave and know you deserve.

Life is not about getting things. It's about becoming something. And true success in life comes when we recognize that.

As surprising as this may seem, true success is metaphysical. It's about satisfying our innermost needs. It's about finding significance and connectedness through what we give. It's not about the symbols we collect or the attention we attract.

To quote legendary NCAA basketball coach John Wooden, "Success is peace of mind, which is a direct result of self-satisfaction in knowing you did your best to become the best you are capable of becoming."[5]

SUCCEEDING THROUGH FAILURE

Still, there's something holding us back.

Failure.

Most of us have been trained to see failures as a detour to success. Ideally, we think, we should not fail on the way to our goals. We have all heard stories of those elite few who seem to have the magic touch, who never seem to stumble, the "best of the best."

The problem is that there is no such thing and no such person. The best typically fail the most. Why? Because failure isn't a detour from success; failure, in fact, is the only path to success. As Winston Churchill once said, "Success is walking from failure to failure with no loss of enthusiasm."[6]

If we want to achieve vertical success, we have to change how we see failure.

When you live in a world of symbols and attention, failure is daunting. If you're pursuing symbols of success, failure means you didn't get the trophy you worked for. And if you're all about attention, your image is so crucial that any failure must be avoided;

there's no time when you cannot be perfect or your image will be shattered.

To people who are self-focused, failure is to be avoided at all costs. You hope to get to your destination as quickly and painlessly as possible in order to show others (and yourself) that you're a success. To self-centered people, life always needs to work out in their favor, and if any external circumstance doesn't materialize in the way they expected, they really feel it. They are not free. They live in an emotional prison. Their thoughts, feelings, and emotions are subject to and dependent upon everything around them.

However, when your life is about giving—when you recognize that the journey is more important than the destination and that you are just a work in progress, and when you tap into your inner 3-year-old and allow yourself to be vulnerable—you quickly realize that failure allows you to engage in the one thing that'll make you great.

And that is deliberate practice.

DELIBERATE PRACTICE MAKES PERFECT

In Chapter 4, I mentioned the 10,000-hour rule, a concept popularized by Malcolm Gladwell in his book *Outliers*.[7] That idea should make more sense to us now because we know that neuroplasticity orients your brain around an activity, and the more you do something, the stronger the neuroconnections will get. Hence, we see how practicing something for 10,000 hours will lead to mastery.

However, developing an expertise requires more than just hours of practice. It requires, as Anders Ericsson, PhD, professor of psychology at Florida State University, said, hours of "deliberate practice."[8]

We assume that if you engage in an activity again and again, you'll get better at it. But Dr. Ericsson asked, "What if you're reinforcing bad habits? What if you are making mistakes and repeating those mistakes? You'll wind up becoming an expert in doing things the wrong way!"

Think about the simple habit of brushing your teeth. We know that if you brush every day, it will become second nature to you, because through neuroplasticity, you strengthen the neuroconnections involved with brushing your teeth. But what if you're brushing wrong? What if you're brushing too hard or too soft or too quickly, and you're not actually cleaning your teeth? Then you're creating neuroconnections, but they're not neuroconnections for greatness, they're for mediocrity.

Deliberate practice sets the bar higher. It posits that when you repeat an action, you shouldn't just do it. You should do it in a deliberate way. You should analyze your performance, see what you're doing right and wrong, and figure out what can be improved—whether it's with your sales call, your swing, the way you treated that patient, or how you analyzed the data. You have to constantly tweak your performance to enhance the nuances of your skill. Then, with the requisite number of hours, will you get better.

We see this with language development in children. When they start talking, they get words half right, and Mom or Dad corrects them until they fully get it. For example, at breakfast time, my son used to ask for "Chee-yos." Everyone would think it was really cute, but my wife would gently correct him, "Cheerios. Cheer-ee-ohs." She would do this on a regular basis, every time he mispronounced the word. As he got older, he eventually figured it out, moving from "Chee-yos" to "Cheer-os" and finally to "Cheerios."

My wife and son were engaged in a form of deliberate practice. My son did the basics. He recognized the word *Cheerios* as representing the cereal he loved the most. He formed neuroconnections between the food and the word, but those connections were flawed. So his mom helped him enhance those connections until he got it right.

Wouldn't life be amazing if you had your mom (or maybe a coach like John Wooden) walking around with you all day to nudge you in the right direction?

Well, guess what? Life does that already. Life has a way of showing you what you're doing wrong: It's called failure. Failure is incredible, because failure can actually help you get better.

Failure shows you where you're off. It shows you which rituals need adjustment. Failure shows you the areas of your life you could get better at. And if you're looking at life from the perspective of the journey, you get excited to adapt, to modify, to revise—so that over time, you can become better and better and better.[9]

If you see your life as one of deliberate practice, you are completely free. If you succeed, that's great! But should you feel unsuccessful, blocked, or let down, then that "failure" allows you to learn something that you could never have learned otherwise—and that is great, too.

Thomas Edison, the man who invented the lightbulb, was one of the world's greatest innovators. But he only got there after many failures. His teachers said he was "too stupid to learn anything,"[10] and he was fired from his first two jobs for not being productive enough. But he didn't view these things as setbacks—he saw them as ways to grow. He used failure as a resource for research and as a way to better understand his product and consumers. It took 1,000 failed attempts before he was able to invent the lightbulb. When a reporter asked how it felt to fail 1,000 times, Edison replied, "I didn't fail 1,000 times. The lightbulb was an invention with 1,000 steps." [11]

That is true freedom.

When you don't need the world to tell you how great you are in order to feel great; when you don't need external approval to feel successful; when you recognize that you don't need to take or to get, but instead to give and to grow—then you are truly free. Free to live in the now. Free to take every single moment to learn from life and get better.

Life is about being more than you were yesterday. And it's when you go all-in on every step of the journey that life begins to feel awesome.

Here is an exercise I have people do. They list their failures and try to learn a lesson from each one. Then they create a ritual around a deliberate adjustment so that they can habituate that lesson into their lives.

EXERCISE VI—DELIBERATE PRACTICE

FAILURE	LESSON	ADAPTATION
Boss was upset that my assignment wasn't done in time.	Be more communicative with regards to my deliverables.	Every time I get an assignment, ask for his/her expectation of timing.
When I made my presentation, I spoke too fast and people didn't follow what I was saying.	When you are nervous, you speak fast; work to slow down.	Before you start each speech, smile and take a deep breath. When you feel yourself going too fast, stop for a drink and slow your mind down.
I cheated on my diet, again.	I have little discipline at night when I get home from work, especially if I'm stressed.	After dinner, leave the kitchen and finish my night in my bedroom.
I was too distracted to be present with my kids.	When you get home, you still have too much on your mind; you need to gain perspective of what's important.	When you arrive home, keep all electronic devices in a drawer. "Cross over" from work to focus just on the kids.

For a downloadable copy of this chart, go to charlieharary.com/book.

BACK TO "OUR MINDS SHAPE REALITY"

Enhancing our minds is what this book is all about. But let's go a step further.

Stoic philosophy tells us that there are no good or bad events in life, only our perception of events. William Shakespeare turned to this same sentiment in Hamlet: ". . . for there is nothing either good or bad, but thinking makes it so."[12] Famed psychologist Albert Ellis used this idea to form the basis of cognitive behavioral therapy, which is now the dominant method for helping people overcome problems ranging from depression to anxiety to anger.[13]

The negativity we feel, those emotions that hold us back from becoming the people we want to be, are caused by our schemas. Why? As we've discussed, it's because our minds shape our reality. The feelings you have are not based on the circumstances around you. Your interpretation of events is what makes you feel a certain way. How you *see* the world impacts how you *feel* about it. Events don't upset you. Your perception of those events upsets you.

Change your perception, and you change your feelings.

In 1997, Joe Tomaka, PhD, and his colleagues at the University of Texas at El Paso did a study on how we perceive stressful situations and their impact on our response.[14] The study suggested that our cognitive appraisal of something, the way we see it, impacts our response to it. So whether we see a stressful event as a threat or a challenge will alter how we react to it. Even if we are experiencing the same situation, our mental interpretation of the event will determine our emotional response. By turning a threat into an opportunity, we can make a major shift in how we feel and how we are able to deal with it.

Why? Because circumstances are neutral. They don't come with emotion. They don't have an attached feeling. We give the circumstances the feeling. That comes from us.

If you miss your flight, that's neutral information. You may be upset about the inconvenience that it causes, but that's just your perception of the information. You could decide to be excited that you missed your flight so you can spend some extra time in the airport's new shopping concourse or catch up on the book you've been meaning to read while you wait for the next flight. You could think more fatalistic thoughts—that maybe if you'd made the flight, something terrible would've happened at the other end, and this delay in your plans is God's blessing.

What I'm saying is that missing the flight wasn't factually a "bad" thing. Missing the flight isn't what gets you upset. The event itself is neutral. What gets you upset is your belief about how the world is supposed to work. When that belief is shattered by something that's out of your control, it leaves you feeling disempowered.

To be able to utilize this information, try to imagine some "typical" life scenarios. Leave out, for now, moments of extreme joy or pain, and picture the more frequent, everyday situations in life. Picture a situation that you are going through or went through. Realize that whatever happened to you is emotionally neutral. It doesn't come with a feeling attached to it. Once the information gets processed through your schema, you start to feel something.

When our expectations don't materialize, we get disappointed. When life doesn't go our way, why do we get upset? It's because we thought "it's supposed to." But that's just a belief. Who told us that everything is supposed to go our way or that we have a right to expect that from the world?

Happy people don't have better lives. What they have are better beliefs. Their lives aren't different. They miss flights, too. What's different are their schemas.

By now, assuming you've read the previous chapters in this book, you know that you can change your schemas. You also know that if you want to enhance your experience in life, it's not about working on your circumstances—changing your job, seeking out thrills, avoiding problems—it's about changing your mind.

Circumstances do not determine the quality of your life. Circumstances are correlative; they are a factor, maybe a big factor in your experience, but there is a missing piece that is more directly connected to how you feel and how you experience life. That piece is your mind. It's your mental processing mechanism. By understanding the power of your mind and the needs of your soul, you can learn to process any circumstance in the most empowering way.

EVERLASTING EMPOWERMENT

We all feel disempowered. We all feel anxiety, fear, and embarrassment. How are we supposed to overcome the myriad negative emotions that seem to hijack our lives?

If you're a plumber trying to find a leak, and you walk into a room and see water leaking from the ceiling, that's good news because you can trace where that water is coming from and get to the bottom of the problem.

In life, be like that plumber: Use the information you're given as a starting point to engage in deliberate practice to constantly improve your schema. Ask yourself: Why do I feel disempowered? Why do I feel threatened? Anxious? Nervous? What belief can I adjust so that the next time I encounter this circumstance, I can feel more resilient? What new ritual can I include in my day to enable me to feel more empowered the next time I'm in this room or I see that person or I get up on stage to speak?

Try to imagine a life in which, during empowering moments, you're all-in in the moment, and during disempowering moments, you are engaged in the deliberate practice to get better.

DOUG AND STACY

To say that Doug and Stacy were overwhelmed was an understatement. Doug was the manager of a popular restaurant, and Stacy was a physical therapist. They lived very busy lives. Between their schedules, obligations, and juggling everything on their plate, they felt like they never had a moment to breathe.

They were high school sweethearts who got engaged in college and married soon after graduation. They put off having a family because they couldn't imagine how they would find the time or the money. As fate would have it, Stacy got pregnant and had not one, but two bundles of joy—twin boys.

When we spoke, the boys were about a year and a half old, and this couple was drowning. There were times, Stacy said, when she felt like she couldn't breathe for hours on end. She would wake up in the middle of the night in pure panic. Doug said that there were times after work when he got in his car and just drove because he needed the quiet time so badly.

The two of them felt completely disempowered. This led to bickering, complaining, and blaming, which strained their marriage.

"We all feel disempowered at times," I said. "If you're living life to its fullest, you're going to have moments where you feel overwhelmed."

We went through the research on stress, and I explained the difference between circumstance and experience, how our circumstances are inherently neutral and how our schemas are what color situations with emotions. When I was done, there was a silence on the other end of the line. Finally, Doug said, "That all sounds great, but what can we do today to feel better?"

It was time to get practical. So I shared with them an exercise that I do myself on a fairly regular basis.

"As you go through your day, you're going to experience one of two core feelings: empowered or disempowered. These emotions will either give you more strength or sap you of it. Feeling empowered means that your mind has aligned itself in the optimal way to grapple with what's in front of it. Either it's enjoying the good you've been given or it's overcoming the challenge you've been presented with. If you feel that way, lean into that feeling more. Allow yourself to feel the empowerment more fully, to be present in that emotion. Go with it through the action.

However, plenty of times in your day you'll feel disempowered. You'll want to give up, you'll feel there's no hope. When you're feeling that way, please don't analyze it or react to it. Just continue doing what you're doing, and take note of where you were when you felt that way. Then, at the end of the day, look back at all the moments of disempowerment and write down the following three things: where you were, how you felt, and why."

Here is the chart I sent them to get started.

EXERCISE VII—UNDERSTANDING EMOTIONS

FEELING	WHERE ARE YOU?	WHY?
Overwhelmed	Monday morning at work	So much to do
Guilty	At home at the end of the night	When I am home, I feel like should be working, and when I am working, I feel like I should be at home.
Anxiety	Driving to the restaurant	Because I need to perform at a high level today
Hopeless	Dining room table, paying bills	We keep working but don't have enough to cover our living expenses and save for the future.

For a downloadable copy of this chart, go to charlieharary.com/book.

Stacy and Doug called me back a week later. "We've been working on the list," Stacy said, "and now we can better articulate how we are feeling, but that doesn't help us feel better."

I moved on to part two. I told them to take their lists and add a column, and ask each other for advice they would give someone else in the same situation. Then write down that advice.

EXERCISE VIII—UNDERSTANDING EMOTIONS II

FEELING	WHERE ARE YOU?	WHY?	ADVICE YOU WOULD GIVE SOMEONE ELSE
Overwhelmed	Monday morning at work	So much to do	You don't have to do it all. Just take it one day at a time.
Guilty	At home at the end of the night	When I am home, I feel like I should be working, and when I am working, I feel like I should be at home.	You're working for your kids; there is no one way to parent. Enjoy them when you are with them.
Anxiety	Driving to the restaurant	Because I need to perform at a high level today	You are good at your job. Focus on all the positive feedback you have received over the years. Just focus on giving people a good experience.
Hopeless	Dining room table, paying bills	We keep working but don't have enough to cover our living expenses and save for the future.	We're covering our expenses, and that's great in today's economy. Life is expensive, and we should take a minute to enjoy the things we are trying so hard to afford.

For a downloadable copy of this chart, go to charlieharary.com/book.

"If you do this for a few weeks, you will realize that the only reason you have these disempowered feelings is because of some negative belief," I said. "The reason why you feel guilty is because you want to be a perfect parent when there are no perfect parents. The reason why you're anxious is because you're scared about the future, but no one is in control of the future. The reason why you're overwhelmed is because you think you have to do everything right now, but you really don't. You just have to do one thing right now.

By writing down someone else's advice and making it our own, we see it more clearly.

Behavioral economist Dan Ariely, PhD, explains that when we give advice to ourselves, we're too emotionally invested and too distracted by our own thoughts and feelings to see the problem from a rational perspective. When we give advice to others, we have less emotional investment and so can see the circumstances more objectively.[15]

The fact is, I do this exercise all the time. I write down all my negative feelings and then ask somebody—usually my wife—for advice on how to deal with it. Or, if I'm alone, I pretend I'm giving my advice to someone else. I disassociate from myself and my own emotions, and I share the type of advice I would give to a friend or loved one.

When I'm able to articulate when and why I'm feeling disempowered—and see the advice I would give to someone else about how to handle it—I'm able to see that my negative beliefs are mostly unfounded. Then? Since it's laid out in front of me, I'm able to work logically to try to get rid of them.

I'm overwhelmed Monday morning because I feel like I need to do everything that day, even though I don't. I have a whole week's worth of time to dig into my to-do list. I feel fear when I get up to speak because I think everyone's judging me, but they're not; the audience wants me to win, and I know from experience that people are always much happier with my presentations than I am. I feel anxiety when I'm traveling because I feel the need to always be productive, and travel slows down my prescheduled day. But I can be just as productive in traffic or a long line if I plan ahead (bring along books, podcasts, etc.).

Try this exercise for yourself. If you stick with it (start as a ritual and make it a habit), you'll see when you work systematically through your moments of disempowerment, just how much your perspective can change. (You already know the reason why.)

As a postscript, as I'm writing this book, Doug and Stacy's twins are now 3. Life may not be a whole lot easier for them, but it sure is a whole lot more enjoyable. The circumstances around them are as hectic, if not more hectic, than ever. But they breathe easier. They've been able to separate the circumstance from the experience in their lives. They've been able to embrace the chaos and realize just how fortunate they are to have each other. They're able to lean on each other for advice and support, and to see the world the way *they* want to see it, rather than the other way around. They are married to each other, they have a family, they have great jobs that they love—they have everything they ever wanted. Only now, they're able to see it without being overwhelmed by it. They're able to live better, because they've gained a new perspective.

And that has made all the difference.

THE GOLDEN LEVER

Viktor Frankl, PhD, the founder of logotherapy, is one of the most inspiring characters of the last half century. After surviving the Holocaust, he went on to write the bestselling book *Man's Search for Meaning*, which has been translated into 35 languages and sold millions of copies. In it, he details the psychological discoveries he made while living in an environment in which most of humanity would simply crumble.

Frankl emerged from the concentration camps with a new understanding of human behavior. What he realized as the Nazis stripped everything away from him—while he lived in just about the least autonomous circumstances anyone ever could—was this: "Between stimulus and response there is a space. In that space is our power to choose our response. In our response lies our growth and our freedom."[16] In an environment where others controlled how and where he slept, what he ate, what he did, whether he lived or died—everything—Frankl realized that his ability to choose his response to his environment was still present. How he responded to the orders given to him and the conditions forced upon him were (to go back to the Self-Determination Theory) the essence of autonomy in action.

In expressing that autonomy, he found his freedom.

Freedom doesn't mean waking up in the morning and doing whatever you want. Freedom means having the character and strength to respond in the way you want to the stimulus in front you. It's not running away from what's happening to us, it's going deeper within ourselves to choose the way we react to it.

That ability, that freedom, which each of us has within us, is what I referred to way back at the very beginning of this book as the "golden lever."

A lever is basically just a long stick that you push or pull to move an object. It's mostly used to move something heavy or make something go fast. While it's a simple tool, if placed and used correctly, it gives you exponentially more power and force than you would otherwise have.

There is a massive world out there that we can't control. There is an equally immense world inside our brains and bodies that can't be easily manipulated. And yet, we yearn for some harmony between these two great entities. Life as we know it is about the time our bodies spend in the world. And we want that time to feel a certain way. We want our life experience to be not only good but great.

To approach either of these entities—the world or our bodies/

brains—directly is imprudent. We aren't strong enough, powerful enough, or disciplined enough to succeed. But we have a tool in our shed: the lever. The lever multiplies our strength. The lever enables us to do what we couldn't do alone.

That lever, the golden lever, is our perspective. It's how we see the world. It's the one part of our lives that we can control. Our attention, our focus, our schema. It's how we process circumstances, and only in the processing of circumstance do we find the life experience we crave. Our circumstances don't give us our desired life experience, our minds do. Our minds constantly adapt and adjust. They shape our reality. They give access to our souls.

When you fully appreciate the power you have over your mind, everything changes. You can upgrade your schemas, create new neuroconnections, and gain control over your emotions and actions. You can direct your life not only where you want it to go, but where you need it to go: toward meaning and purpose, toward transcendence, toward your ideal self. You can direct it, through practical tools, to bypass the traps of endless consumption and momentary gratification and of arrogance and attention, which always leave us feeling empty. You can create a new vision of what you want and ritualize the path toward it, crossing over to all areas of life.

That's when you'll realize that greatness is not something you become, but something you reveal. It is already inside you. You just have to unlock it. It's your choice how to respond to challenges, how to live in the moment, and whether you will fight for excellence in everything you do.

When you make that choice, when you engage in this quest, you will find yourself no longer lacking and no longer unsatisfied—because you will understand what you need and be far too immersed in the journey, far too inspired by the possibility of growing each day, and far too enveloped by the Unifying Energy you feel when you connect to the people in your life to wallow in not having it quite yet.

That is when you will feel alive and satisfied in every way—because you'll finally be living the soul-satisfying, need-fulfilling, lifelong journey of becoming the true you that you were always meant to be.

And that, to answer the question we started with, I believe, is "what you want."

EPILOGUE

NEVER STOP

I'm done."

"No, you're not."

"No, really, I'm wiped."

"You still have more in you."

"No, seriously, I know me, and I'm *spent*."

"No. We're not done yet. You still have a few more reps in you, so get back on the bench!"

This is a conversation I have regularly with my trainer. (Yes, I caved and got one.) Despite my all-too-common protests, he has the good sense to focus on my muscles and not my whining. When this happens, I relent, and 20 minutes later I realize he was right: I had more in me than I thought.

Our minds aren't conditioned for success. They're conditioned to avoid pain and discomfort. That's why it's so difficult for us to change, even when we know what we want and what we need.

As you finish this book, your mind will likely protest the next steps. Your schema will present you with compelling reasons to avoid putting anything you've read into practice. Some of those reasons will show up now, some may come later, but let me lay out seven of them just so you'll recognize them.

1. "I'VE HEARD THESE IDEAS ALREADY."

We mistake being familiar with an idea with understanding its potential effectiveness. I am sure you've heard of some of the ideas in these pages already. You may have even tried them before. This may lead you to believe that since they haven't helped you in the past, they won't help you going forward. That's not true. Maybe you heard these concepts at a different point in your life, in a different context, or presented in a different way. If something is familiar and it feels true, then maybe now is the time to invest the effort to see if it can be effective for you.

2. "DO I REALLY NEED THIS?"

Status quo is powerful. Really powerful. One of the most misunderstood adages is, "If it ain't broke, don't fix it." Is that the advice we want to live by? "My life is mostly fine, so why put myself through pain to get to more?" I experience that thought every time I go to the gym. "Do I really need this? I'm married with kids. I'm not a bodybuilder. I'm not a professional athlete. Why put myself through this pain just to have better abs?"

Greatness isn't something to pick and choose. It's a path in life. Everything you do should have the same high standard. The fight for excellence is what gives life meaning. You're not sweating for somebody else; you are doing it for yourself. It should encompass how you approach your body, your family, and your life.

3. "IF I CHANGE, I'LL LOSE PEOPLE I'M CLOSE TO."

We all seem to have certain people around us who like to keep us as we are. When we start to grow, it threatens them, so they mock or insult us—whether it's because our change doesn't make sense to them, or they don't appreciate how important the change is, or even because deep down they feel less when we make ourselves more. It's nothing you did; it's just how some people are.

Have you ever sat at dinner with friends and ordered the "healthy" option, only to get the "Oh, come on, live a little" looks? Have you ever tried to disengage from gossiping about a mutual friend? How did *that* go? Many times, our personal growth conflicts with our relationships, and we know it. But here's the thing— life is too short to spend your time nurturing insecure and small-minded people. When you set a standard for yourself, and when it's from a place of genuine desire to be better, the people who love you will support you. At first, they may be scared to lose you, but when they see your growth, your happiness, and your life satisfaction, they will be proud (and inspired). You may lose some friends along the way, but true friends want what's best for each other—and maybe a little personal growth is an effective way to figure out who those friends really are.

4. "IT'S SOMEONE ELSE'S FAULT."

We don't take enough responsibility for our lives. We think that our challenges, our bad habits, our insecurities and weaknesses are the products of other people or circumstances. It's much easier to think that we are not to blame for the lack of satisfaction in our lives. It's our parents, genes, spouse, kids, bosses, employees, in-laws, the economy, or the government that is at fault.

The thing is, we don't fully appreciate that blaming others is toxic. It poisons our minds. It weakens us by conditioning us to be helpless. While we may feel relief for a few minutes, denying responsibility ultimately hurts us and prevents us from growing. Yes, life may have dumped some horrible circumstances on you, but what you do with those circumstances is entirely up to you. Just you. No one else. You may get help from others, but no one else is responsible for your life—only *you*.

Taking full responsibility for every aspect of your life is daunting but liberating. By cutting off your typical excuses, you will create a platform for building a new future.

5. "THERE IS A HACK FOR THIS."

It's important to be smart and efficient, but we are so scared of working hard that we immediately look for shortcuts, gimmicks, or quick-fix pills. If you want to accomplish something that has value, it will cost you. Sometimes it's money, but usually it's time, effort, and commitment. Nothing of real value is free or quick.

We've spent too much time seeing shortcuts portrayed on-screen and even in the books we read. We watch movies where the protagonist goes from rags to riches in 90 minutes. We read biographies that span whole decades in a few pages, and magazine articles that gloss over the untold hours the subject spent practicing his or her craft. The compressed time we've grown accustomed to seeing in our years of being entertained doesn't reflect reality. Time and effort are required for greatness.

Even in this book, it may look like the people who changed their lives did so in the time it took you to read about them doing it. But it didn't. It took them hours, weeks, and months. They're still working on themselves to this day and will hopefully continue.

Life isn't about getting something, it's about *being* something. Instead of focusing your effort on the quickest way, focus it on the best way. You'll be much more satisfied in the end.

6. "I DON'T REALLY DESERVE IT."

Many of us feel we do not deserve to be great. We love to hear stories of "regular" people who through hard work and persistence achieved something special, but deep down we don't believe it could be us. Greatness is for somebody else. We'd *know* if we were special, and we're not. So why endure the toil?

Where does this feeling come from? For some, it's what they heard in their homes. For others, it was from school. For most, it's due to years (or 10,000 hours) of watching people who look perfect on-screen. Every outfit looks great, every line is said at the exact right moment, and life seems to always work out in the end. You know why? Because it's not real. It's amazing what great scriptwriters, a ton of makeup, and lots of editing can do for a person. Real life is messy. It's inelegant. And no one is perfect.

You have been blessed with a Divine spark and a nearly endless capacity to keep going, stretching, far beyond what you think you are capable of right now. That is *special*. You are special. Believe it and act like it.

7. "THIS IS GOING TO BE TOO HARD."

When you look too far ahead, the road seems impossible to traverse. There is so much to do that your desired life may seem miles away. The picture of what the end looks like may seem so unrealistic that it feels unwise to even start.

Remember that a "goal" is only a direction in which to walk, not something you have to reach. Growth doesn't require years, months, or weeks. Growth requires one day at a time. What matters is whether you will make today as great as it can be. That's it. One foot in front of the next, living in the N.O.W.

It will be hard. There will be obstacles. You will lose your inspiration and exhaust your limited willpower. You're going to get knocked down, and when you do, there may not be anyone to pick you up. Just keep moving, however slow. One foot in front of the next. Every day, forever.

Greatness doesn't come to the fastest or strongest, but to the person who is always willing to get up *one more time*.

Greatness is a choice. You have to *choose* to unlock the greatness within. Sometimes all it takes is turning a simple key. Sometimes it takes a hatchet. Sometimes it takes a mound of TNT. And sometimes it just takes the persistence of being there, knocking again and again until that door finally opens.

Of course, once it opens, there will always be another door. And that's the fun of it.

I hope you'll use this book as your personal compass in your journey. I hope you'll reach for it again and again, to be reminded of the incredible capacity and power you have within to change, and change for good. Because believe me, you have within you the ability to be absolutely incredible.

When you choose to keep pushing, even when you think you're fully spent, you'll find that you have far more to give than you ever imagined possible. As always, please feel free to reach out to me anytime at charlie@charlieharary.com.

ACKNOWLEDGMENTS

To Dena, my partner in life. All I have is because of you. "Thank you" doesn't do it justice. The classes, seminars, speeches, and book writing were all possible because of your unwavering love and support.

To my parents, for enduring the challenges of my teenage years and for being both role models and rocks of support, always.

To my grandparents, whose very lives constantly inspire me.

To my children. You are the greatest gifts in the world. Thanks for making life fun, meaningful, and exhausting. And thank you for the constant stream of great material.

To Nena Madonia Oshman and the Dupree Miller team, for believing in me and this concept. For being a friend, advocate, sounding board, and advisor.

To Mark Dagostino, my writing partner. From our first cup of coffee, it has been an honor and a pleasure to work hand in hand with you to make this book a reality. Thank you for the late nights, long voice messages, and endless drafts. Your contribution to this book was beyond just your eloquent pen; it was in your patience, resilience, and desire for excellence.

To Leah Miller, Mark Weinstein, and the entire Rodale team, for giving me this chance to share my passion. Leah, thank you for pushing me to get better, and clearer, and doing so with grace, warmth, and compassion. Mark, thank you for your guidance, insight, and enthusiasm, and for navigating me through uncharted waters with skill, support, and unwavering dedication. To Susan Turner, Brianne Sperber, Anna Cooperberg, Trisha de Guzman, and everyone who contributed along this journey. I am forever grateful. Thank you.

To Rabbi Moshe Weinberger, my guide, mentor, and spiritual advisor. Your words navigate me through the labyrinth of spirituality and inspire me to always strive to be more connected to truth, meaning, and purpose. Thank you.

To Rabbi Shmuel Braun, my metaphysical consultant. Thank you for ensuring that the depth of these words remained concise and accurate, and for guiding me through such enchanted forests.

To Jason Barnett, for pushing me to be my best at everything I do. To Scott Rechler and the RXR team, for embodying the principle of doing good while doing well.

To Henry Kauftheil, for believing in this from the first moment. Your vision, capacity, and strength constantly inspire me.

To Hayah Rafie, thank you for your tireless efforts and invaluable assistance with this book and my daily life.

To Marissa Leifer, for your assistance with the book and for connecting me to Mark and Nena.

To all my family and friends for your constant support, love, and dedication, as well as for reviewing the book, providing insights, and helping me develop this material. Thank you for all that you do and for all that you mean to me.

To Hashem, for giving me more than I could have dreamed. I hope this book makes you proud.

ENDNOTES

INTRODUCTION

1   Laura A. Pratt, Debra J. Brody, and Qiuping Gu, "Antidepressant Use in Persons Aged 12 and Over: United States, 2005–2008," *NCHS Data Brief* no. 76 (October 2011), https://www.cdc.gov/nchs/data/databriefs/db76.pdf.

2   Ibid.

3   Ibid.

4   T. S. Eliot, *The Rock* (London: Faber & Faber, 1934).

CHAPTER 1

1   Rosenthal's theories were attacked by several prestigious scholars, one of whom was Columbia University's Robert Thorndike, who claimed, "Pygmalion is so defective technically that one can only regret that it ever got beyond the eyes of the original investigators!" In addition, the founder of the United Federation of Teachers, Albert Shanker, criticized Rosenthal in the *New York Times*, mocking his results. See K. Ellison, "Being Honest about the Pygmalion Effect," *Discover*, December 2015, http://discovermagazine.com/2015/dec/14-great-expectations.

2   Mike Hockney, *How to Create the Universe* (Lulu Press, 2016).

3   The Oak School was the name he used for the research report. The school's name was the Spruce Elementary School in South San Francisco, California.

4   R. Rosenthal and L. Jacobson, "Pygmalion in the Classroom," *Urban Review* 3, no. 1 (1968): 16–20.

5   Ibid.

6   The knowledge that you can improve your intelligence actually impacts achievement. Dr. Carol Dweck taught a group of grade school students how to have a "growth" mind-set, and gaining that perspective enabled them to improve their grades as opposed to peer students in the control group who, without such perspective, displayed a downward trajectory in grades. See

L. S. Blackwell, K. H. Trzesniewski, and C. S. Dweck, "Implicit Theories of Intelligence Predict Achievement across an Adolescent Transition: A Longitudinal Study and an Intervention," *Child Development* 78, no. 1 (2007): 246–63.

7   Ellen J. Langer. *Counterclockwise: Mindful Health and the Power of Possibility* (New York: Ballantine Books, 2009). The broadcast in England was entitled: "The Young Ones." For more, see Langer's Web site, http://langermindfulnessinstitute.com/ counterclockwise-research.

8   ROTC is the Reserve Officers' Training Corps. It's a college course designed to help students build leadership skills for a military or civilian career and also enables students who want to serve in the United States Army to enter as a second lieutenant.

9   E. Langer et al., "Believing Is Seeing: Using Mindlessness (Mindfully) to Improve Visual Acuity," *Psychological Science* 21, no. 5 (May 2010): 661–66.

10 Ibid.

11 A. J. Crum and E. J. Langer, "Mind-Set Matters Exercise and the Placebo Effect," *Psychological Science* 18, no. 2 (2007): 165–71.

CHAPTER 2

1   The concept of reality and our perception of it has been a matter of philosophical debate for generations. Immanuel Kant played a pivotal role in the development of how we understand reality as he bridged the gap between two schools of thought: the rationalists, who believed that knowledge could be attained by reason, and the empiricists, who held that knowledge is experienced through our senses. Kant's theory, called transcendental idealism, posits that both are correct. According to Kant, we cannot know the actual objective world itself, because all of our scientific and mathematical observations pass through the lens of our mind. Kant's theories place the mind in the center—hence the concept of schema, claiming that only through our mental context can we experience things. See Immanuel Kant, *Critique of Pure Reason* (Hamburg: Meiner, 1781); see also Immanuel Kant and Paul Guyer and Allen Wood, eds., *Critique of Pure Reason* (Cambridge: Cambridge University Press, 1998).

In the post-Kantian era, schools of thought such as materialists and idealists emerged. The materialists claimed that reality exists outside our minds even if we never experienced it. The idealists claimed that there is no objective world and that reality exists entirely in our minds. A third school of thought, that of dualism, posits that reality is a combination of both the physical and nonphysical/spiritual. Each person has both; this is the mind and body. For more, see W. Jewell-Lapan, "Perception and Reality," *The Journal of Philosophy* 33, no. 14 (July 1936): 365–73; John W. Yolton, *Perception and Reality: A History from Descartes to Kant* (Ithaca, NY: Cornell University Press, 1996); and D. Rose and D. Brown, "Idealism and Materialism in Perception," *Perception* 44, no. 4 (2015): 423–35.

2   Jean Piaget, *The Child's Conception of the World* (London: Routledge and Kegan Paul Ltd., 1929); see also Jean Piaget, *The Origins of Intelligence in Children* (New York: International Universities Press, 1952).

The concept of schema was popularized through the work of the British psychologist Sir Frederic Bartlett. See his book *Remembering: A Study in Experimental and Social Psychology* (Cambridge: Cambridge University Press, 1932); and the work of Ulric Neisser. See Ulric Neisser, *Cognitive Psychology,* Classic Edition (New York: Psychology Press, 2014).

3   Separately but related, neurologist Sir Henry Head coined the term *body schema,* which was defined as "the impressions produced by incoming sensory impulses in such a way that the final sensation of [body] position, or of locality, rises into consciousness charged with a relation to something that has happened before." See H. Head, "Studies in Neurology," *The American Journal of the Medical Sciences* 164, no. 4 (1922): 601.

4   Jean Piaget, "Piaget's Theory," in *Piaget and His School* (Berlin, Heidelberg: Springer, 1976): 11–23.

5   Ibid.

6   Stereotypes, biases, and prejudices are based on beliefs about groups of people that we have little exposure to. As we increase our exposure to such people, we start to realize the deficiencies in our knowledge and our schema accommodates that information, reducing that original bias.

7   The mental schema has a significant impact on eyewitness testimony and, by extension, the judicial system. For a greater exploration, see C. Laney and E. F. Loftus, "Eyewitness Testimony and Memory Biases," in *Noba Textbook Series: Psychology,* ed. R. Biswas-Diener and E. Diener (Champaign, IL: DEF Publishers, 2017): DOI:nobaproject.com. See also L. Engelhardt, "The Problem with Eyewitness Testimony: A Talk by Barbara Tversky, Professor of Psychology, and George Fisher, Professor of Law," *Stanford Journal of Legal Studies* 1, no. 1 (1999): 25–29; J. W. Alba and L. Hasher, "Is Memory Schematic?" *Psychological Bulletin* 93, no. 2 (1983): 203–31; and W. F. Brewer and J. C. Treyens, "Role of Schemata in Memory for Places," *Cognitive Psychology* 13, no. 2 (April 1981): 207–30.

CHAPTER 3

1   The story of Rajesh Malik is in the 2009 documentary, *The Plastic Fantastic Brain*, written by Elizabeth Trojian and directed by Robin Bicknell.

2   The most recent product is the BrainPort V100. It's a video camera mounted on a pair of sunglasses with a wire to the tongue and a handheld controller that enables adjustment, zoom, contrast, etc. The camera operates in diverse lighting environments. It contains 400 electrodes that stimulate the tongue, increasing the field of vision. For more information, see http://www.wicab.com/brainport-v100.

3   Alfred Binet and Suzanne Heisler, trans., *Modern Ideas about Children* (Menlo Park, CA: Suzanne Heisler, 1975): 105–6.

4   Norman Doidge, *The Brain That Changes Itself: Stories of Personal Triumph from the Frontiers of Brain Science* (New York: Penguin, 2007).

5   Ibid., xv–xvi.

6   S. Herculano-Houzel, "The Human Brain in Numbers: A Linearly Scaled-Up Primate Brain," *Frontiers in Human Neuroscience* 3 (2009): 31.

7   Addison Greenwood, *Science at the Frontier*, vol. 1 (National Academies Press, 1992): chapter 9.

8   Rita Smilkstein, *We're Born to Learn: Using the Brain's Natural Learning Process to Create Today's Curriculum* (Thousand Oaks, CA: Corwin Press, 2011).

9   Donald O. Hebb, *The Organization of Behavior: A Neuropsychological Theory* (New York: John Wiley & Sons, 1949). In his monumental book, Hebb stated, "When an axon of cell *A* is near enough to excite a cell *B* and repeatedly or persistently takes part in firing it, some growth process or metabolic change takes place in one or both cells such that *A*'s efficiency, as one of the cells firing *B*, is increased."

However, American neurobiologist Carla Shatz, PhD, is credited with coining the famous phrase in an article published in *Scientific American*. See C. J. Shatz, "The Developing Brain," *Scientific American* 267, no. 3 (1992): 60–67.

10   Doidge, *The Brain That Changes Itself*.

11   The sources for Arrowsmith's story include: Barbara Arrowsmith-Young, *The Woman Who Changed Her Brain: How I Left My Learning Disability Behind and Other Stories of Cognitive Transformation* (New York: Simon & Schuster Paperbacks, 2013); "TEDxToronto 2012 Talk:

Barbara Arrowsmith-Young," TED Talk, www.tedxtoronto.com/talks/tedxtoronto-2012-talk-barbara-arrowsmith-young/; and the 2008 documentary, *The Brain That Changes Itself.* For more, see also www.barbaraarrowsmithyoung.com.

12 "TEDxToronto 2012 Talk: Barbara Arrowsmith-Young."

13 Amanda Hooton, "Can Barbara Arrowsmith-Young's Cognitive Exercises Change Your Brain?" *The Sydney Morning Herald,* April 22, 2007, www.smh.com.au/good-weekend/can-barbara-arrowsmithyoungs-cognitive-exercises-change-your-brain-20170419-gvnsn5.html.

14 Aleksandr R. Luria, *The Man with a Shattered World: The History of a Brain Wound* (New York: Basic Books, 1972).

15 Jon Henley, "How Barbara Arrowsmith-Young Rebuilt Her Own Brain," *The Guardian,* June 12, 2012, https://www.theguardian.com/science/2012/jun/12/barbara-arrowsmith-young-rebuilt-brain.

16 Ibid. In this interview, she said, "I read a page of Kierkegaard—because philosophy is obviously very conceptual, so had been impossible for me—and I understood it. I read pages from 10 books, and every single one I understood. I was like, hallelujah! It was like stepping from darkness into light."

17 "TEDxToronto 2012 Talk: Barbara Arrowsmith-Young."

18 For additional information on how practicing skills can reshape the brain, see Will Storr, "Can You Think Yourself into a Different Person?" *Mosaic,* November 17, 2015, https://mosaicscience.com/story/neuroplasticity; a study by neuropsychologist Thomas Elbert on string players and how their brains rewired themselves as a result of hours of practice, in T. Elbert et al., "Increased Cortical Representation of the Fingers of the Left Hand in String Players," *Science* 270, no. 5234 (1995): 305–7; and a study by Eleanor Maguire on increased gray matter in one hippocampal area of London's taxi drivers due to their incredible spatial knowledge of the maze of streets, in E. A. Maguire, K. Woollett, and H. J. Spiers, "London Taxi Drivers and Bus Drivers: A Structural MRI and Neuropsychological Analysis," *Hippocampus* 16, no. 12 (2006): 1091–1101.

19 Kelly Marshall, "Born with Half a Brain, Woman Living Full Life," CNN, October 12, 2009, www.cnn.com/2009/HEALTH/10/12/woman.brain.index.html?iref=nextin.

20 Robin Marantz Henig, "Scientist at Work: Benjamin S. Carson; For Many, Pediatric Neurosurgeon Is a Folk Hero," *New York Times,* June 8, 1993.

21 E. P. G. Vining et al., "Why Would You Remove Half a Brain? The Outcome of 58 Children after Hemispherectomy—The Johns Hopkins Experience: 1968 to 1996," *Pediatrics* 100, no. 2 (1997): 163–71; see also M. B. Pulsifer et al., "The Cognitive Outcome of Hemispherectomy in 71 Children," *Epilepsia* 45, no. 3 (2004): 243–54.

22 The quote is from the incredible story of Jody Miller, a girl who suffered from intense epileptic seizures when she was three years old and underwent a hemispherectomy with outstanding results. See *Brain Plasticity—The Story of Jody*, July 3, 2011, https://www.youtube.com /watch?v=VaDlLD97CLM.

23 Doidge, *The Brain That Changes Itself.*

CHAPTER 4

1 Mihaly Csikszentmihalyi, *Flow: The Psychology of Optimal Experience* (New York: Harper & Row, 1990).

2 Ibid.

3 For additional insights on how the brain processes multiple sources of stimuli, see the research by cognitive scientist Colin Cherry known as the "cocktail party effect," which explains how people at a cocktail party can focus on one conversation while limiting their awareness of other conversations. In another study, Cherry also had people wear headphones and instructed them to listen to only one side, ignoring the other. The subjects were often unable to tell what language the speech in the unattended channel was, as most of it was blocked from conscious awareness. See N. L. Wood and N. Cowan, "The Cocktail Party Phenomenon Revisited: Attention and Memory in the Classic Selective Listening Procedure of Cherry (1953)," *Journal of Experimental Psychology: General* 124, no. 3 (1995): 243–62.

4 William James, *The Principles of Psychology* (New York: Dover Publications, 1950): 402.

5 For more on the ill effects of multitasking, see N. K. Napier, "The Myth of Multitasking," *Psychology Today,* May 12, 2014, https://www .psychologytoday.com/blog/creativity-without-borders/201405/the-myth -multitasking; see also E. Ophir, C. Nass, and A. D. Wagner, "Cognitive Control in Media Multitaskers," *Proceedings of the National Academy of Sciences* 106, no. 37 (2009): 15583–587.

6 K. Cherry, "How Does Attention Work?" *Verywell,* April 10, 2015, https://www.verywell.com/how-does-attention-work-2795015.

7   James, *Principles of Psychology*, 423.

8   This concept has been found repeatedly in materials relating to positive psychology. See Tal Ben-Shahar, *Even Happier: A Gratitude Journal for Daily Joy and Lasting Fulfillment* (New York: McGraw-Hill, 2010); Shawn Achor, "The Happiness Advantage: Linking Positive Brains to Performance," TEDxTalk, June 30, 2011, https://www.youtube.com /watch?v=GXy__kBVq1M; Janice Kaplan, *The Gratitude Diaries: How a Year Looking on the Bright Side Can Transform Your Life* (New York: Dutton, Penguin Random House, 2015).

9   This is attributed to Tony Robbins. See "Where Focus Goes, Energy Flows," September 10, 2016, https://www.tonyrobbins.com/career-business /where-focus-goes-energy-flows/.

10   Malcolm Gladwell, *Outliers: The Story of Success* (New York: Little, Brown and Co., 2008).

11   Matt Peckham, "Tetris at 30: An Interview with the Historic Puzzle Game's Creator," *Time*, June 6, 2014, http://time.com/2837390/tetris -at-30-pajitnov-interview/.

12   R. J. Haier et al., "Regional Glucose Metabolic Changes after Learning a Complex Visuospatial/Motor Task: A Positron Emission Tomographic Study," *Brain Research* 570, no. 1–2 (1992): 134–43.

13   The cerebral cortex is the outer layer of the brain, also called "gray matter." It's where memory, attention, perception, awareness, thought, language, and consciousness are centered. It's where your neurological connections take place. When we create new connections, we thicken this area of the brain, thereby making it stronger.

14   Haier et al., "Regional Glucose Metabolic Changes."

CHAPTER 5

1   For the impact of dopamine on plasticity, see M. Ishikawa et al., "Dopamine Triggers Heterosynaptic Plasticity," *Journal of Neuroscience* 33, no. 16 (2013): 6759–65.

2   N. M. Avena, P. Rada, and B. G. Hoebel, "Evidence for Sugar Addiction: Behavioral and Neurochemical Effects of Intermittent, Excessive Sugar Intake," *Neuroscience & Biobehavioral Reviews* 32, no. 1 (2008): 20–39.

3   E. L. Deci and R. M. Ryan, "Self-Determination Theory: A Macrotheory of Human Motivation, Development, and Health," *Canadian Psychology* 49, no. 3 (2008): 182–5.

4   Ibid.

5   Jane McGonigal, "Gaming Can Make a Better World," TED Talk, February 2010, https://www.ted.com/talks/jane_mcgonigal_gaming_ can_make_a_better_world

6   A. K. Przybylski, C. S. Rigby, and R. M. Ryan, "A Motivational Model of Video Game Engagement," *Review of General Psychology* 14, no. 2 (2010): 154–66. See also Chris Gayomali, "Psychology: We Play Video Games to Chase Our 'Ideal Selves'," *Time*, August 4, 2011, http://techland.time.com /2011/08/04/psychology-we-play-video-games-to-chase-our-ideal-selves/.

7   "Getting to the Heart of the Appeal of Videogames," Association for Psychological Science, August 3, 2011, https://www.psychologicalscience. org/news/releases/getting-to-the-heart-of-the-appeal-of-videogames.html#. WSspnOvytEY; see also A. K. Przybylski et al., "The Ideal Self at Play: The Appeal of Video Games That Let You Be All You Can Be," *Psychological Science* 23, no. 1 (2012): 69–76.

8   R. M. Ryan and E. L. Deci, "Self-Determination Theory and the Facilitation of Intrinsic Motivation, Social Development, and Well-Being," *American Psychologist* 55, no. 1 (2000): 68–78.

CHAPTER 6

1   See Allison Coudert, *The Impact of the Kabbalah in the Seventeenth Century: The Life and Thought of Francis Mercury van Helmont* (1614–1698) (Leiden, Netherlands: Brill, 1999); Sarah Hutton, *Anne Conway: A Woman Philosopher* (Cambridge: Cambridge University Press, 2004): 140–155; Allison Coudert, "Leibniz, Locke, Newton and the Kabbalah," in *The Christian Kabbalah: Jewish Mystical Books and Their Christian Interpreters*, ed. Joseph Dan (Cambridge: Harvard College Library, 1997): 149–79; Anne Conway, *The Principles of the Most Ancient and Modern Philosophy*, trans. and ed. Allison Coudert and Taylor Corse (Cambridge: Cambridge University Press, 1996); David Bakan, *Sigmund Freud and the Jewish Mystical Tradition* (Mineola, NY: Dover Publications, 2004); and Sanford L. Drob, "Jung and the Kabbalah," *History of Psychology* 2, no. 2 (1999): 102–18.

2   It is important to stress that this Kabbalistic approach is not asserting that the Divine Being is the world but rather that the world is within It. Divinity is present in all things but at the same time transcends it all, is simultaneously immanent, permeating the mundane, and yet transcendent, wholly independent of the material universe. This approach is distinct from that of pantheism. To a pantheist, the Divine and the universe are identical; the Divine is not only in the universe, it is the universe.

In contradistinction, the Kabbalistic approach asserts that although the Divine infinitely transcends the world, there exists a Divine life force, an interconnected unity of energy, that exists in all matter as its essential existence. Because this energy is the truth of existence, humanity has been given the ability and free will to access and create a deeper relationship to this energy through its actions.

For more, see David B. Ruderman, "Jewish Thought in Newtonian England: The Career and Writings of David Nieto (In Memory of Jacob J. Petuchowski)," in *Proceedings of the American Academy for Jewish Research* 58 (1992): 193–219; Rabbi Schneur Zalman of Liadi, *Tanya*, (Brooklyn, 1965); Ba'al Shem Tov, *The Testament of Rabbi Israel Baal Shem Tov* (Kehot Publication Society, 1998); and Shimon Bar Yochai, *Tikunei HaZohar* (Mantua, Italy, 1558).

3   Taken from written correspondence to his friend Marcel Grossman. See E. L. Schucking, review of *Einstein: His Life and Universe*, by Walter Isaacson, *Physics Today* 60, no. 11 (2007): 59.

4   See Stefan Klein. *We Are All Stardust: Scientists Who Shaped Our World Talk about Their Work, Their Lives, and What They Still Want to Know*. New York: Experiment, 2015, 75.

Physicist and bestselling author, Fritjof Capra, PhD, stated, "Quantum theory thus reveals a basic oneness of the universe. It shows that we cannot decompose the world into independently existing smallest units. As we penetrate into matter, nature does not show us any isolated 'building blocks,' but rather appears as a complicated web of relations between the various parts of the whole. These relations always include the observer in an essential way. The human observer constitutes the final link in the chain of observational processes, and the properties of any atomic object can only be understood in terms of the object's interaction with the observe." See Fritjof Capra, *The Tao of Physics* (Boulder, CO, 1975), 68.

While a proper exploration of theoretical physics is well beyond the scope of this work, here are examples of how the quest to unify conflicting laws of nature drives scientific exploration.

William Robert Grove's theory that energy can neither be created or destroyed, rather it can only be transferred (via forces) to other forms of energy, creates a relationship between mechanics, heat, light, electricity, and magnetism by treating them all as manifestations of the same underlying source. See William Robert Grove, *The Correlation of Physical Forces* (London: Longmans, Green, 1874); Hermann von Helmholtz arrived at similar conclusions. See also H. von Helmholtz, "On the Conservation of Force: A Physical Memoir," *Selected Writings of Hermann von Helmholtz* (1847) (Middletown, CT: Wesleyan University Press, 1971): 3–55.

The Higgs boson/God particle is the quantum excitation (higher energy than the ground state) of the Higgs field, a fundamental field believed to permeate the entire Universe. The presence of this field explains why some fundamental particles have mass when they should be massless. This breakthrough discovery gave credence to the presence of the electro-weak and electro-strong forces, and further, the unification of three of the four fundamental forces, the forces that govern the way aspects of our universe interact with each other.

The Grand Unified Theory unifies three of the four fundamental forces. The three forces are then one force "carried" by different methods, which is why the force seemingly manifests as different forces. This is viewed by many as an intermediate step in unifying all four of the fundamental forces into one.

The Theory of Everything attempts to unify all forces, literally everything, into a single force. String theory is one such attempt. String theory attempts to unify the four fundamental forces in the universe, as mentioned above, into one unified theory. In our universe, these fundamental forces appear as four different phenomena, but string theorists believe that in the early universe (when there existed at higher energy levels) these forces are all described by strings interacting with each other.

For more, please see Richard Phillips Feynman, Robert B. Leighton, and Matthew Sands, *The Feynman Lectures on Physics,* Vol. 1 (Boston: Addison Wesley, 1963).

5   See Aldous Huxley, *The Perennial Philosophy* (1st edition) (London: Chatto and Windus, 1946): dust jacket. See also A. Coudert, *The Impact of the Kabbalah in the Seventeenth Century: The Life and Thought of Francis Mercury van Helmont (1614–1698)* (Leiden, The Netherlands: Brill, 1999).

6   *The Hidden Ground of Love: The Letters of Thomas Merton on Religious Experience and Social Concerns*, ed. William H. Shannon (San Diego: Harcourt Brace Jovanovich, 1993).

CHAPTER 7

1   R. Misra and M. McKean, "College Students' Academic Stress and Its Relation to Their Anxiety, Time Management, and Leisure Satisfaction," *American Journal of Health Studies* 16, no. 1 (2000): 41–51.

2   "Data on Behavioral Health in the United States," American Psychological Association, accessed May 27, 2017, www.apa.org /helpcenter/data-behavioral-health.aspx.

3   R. C. Kessler et al., "Age of Onset of Mental Disorders: A Review of Recent Literature," *Current Opinion in Psychiatry* 20, no. 4 (2007): 359–64.

4   Psychologists call this the Scrooge Effect, which posits that mortality reminders make us more generous and prosocial. See E. Jonas et al., "The Scrooge Effect: Evidence That Mortality Salience Increases Prosocial

Attitudes and Behavior," *Personality and Social Psychology Bulletin* 28, no. 10 (2002): 1342–53. See also T. Zaleskiewicz, A. Gasiorowska, and P. Kesebir, "The Scrooge Effect Revisited: Mortality Salience Increases the Satisfaction Derived from Prosocial Behavior," *Journal of Experimental Social Psychology* 59 (2015): 67–76.

5   Joseph Dov Soloveitchik, "The Lonely Man of Faith," *Tradition* 7, no. 2 (1965): 5–67.

6   See David Brooks, "Should You Live for Your Résumé . . . Or Your Eulogy?" TED Talk, 2014, https://www.ted.com/talks/david_brooks _should_you_live_for_your_resume_or_your_eulogy; and N. Linzer et al., "'The Lonely Man of Faith': Implications for Social Work Practice," *Journal of Jewish Communal Service* 83, no. 2–3 (2008): 186–203. In addition, *Time* magazine called the essay "one of the most personal expressions ever voiced by a modern Talmudic authority on the elemental power of religious faith and the ways in which the joy of life often comes mixed with longing, torment, and despair," at www.barnesandnoble.com/w/lonely-man-of-faith -joseph-b-soloveitchik/1100619961#productInfoTabs.

7   Erik H. Erikson, "Elements of a Psychoanalytic Theory of Psychosocial Development," in vol. 1 of *The Course of Life: Psychoanalytic Contributions toward Understanding Personality Development,* ed. Stanley Greenspan and George Pollock (Adelphi, MD: Mental Health Study Center, 1980): 11–61; Martin Heidegger, *Being and Time: A Translation of Sein und Zeit* (Albany, NY: State University of New York Press, 1996); Jean-Paul Sartre, *Being and Nothingness: An Essay on Phenomenological Ontology* (New York: Philosophical Library, 1956); Martin Buber, *Between Man and Man* (New York: Routledge, 2002); Emmanuel Levinas, *Otherwise Than Being or Beyond Essence* (Hague: Kluwer, 1981).

8   See Niccolò Machiavelli, *Art of War* (Chicago: University of Chicago Press, 2005); Thomas Hobbes, *Leviathan* (Oxford: Clarendon Press, 2012); Plato, *The Republic of Plato* (London: Oxford University Press, 1945): vol. 1, 175–203; and Karl Marx and Friedrich Engels, *The Communist Manifesto* (London: Penguin, 2002).

9   Mishnah, *Pirkei Avot* (Ethics of the Fathers), 1:14.

10 Soloveitchik, "Lonely Man of Faith."

11 Ecclesiastes 7:2. The full quote is: "It is better to go to a house of mourning than to go to a house of feasting, because that is the end of every man, and the living takes it to heart."

12 See Ian Fleming, *You Only Live Twice* (United Kingdom: Jonathan Cape, 1964).

13   Tal Ben-Shahar, *The Question of Happiness: On Finding Meaning, Pleasure, and the Ultimate Currency* (iUniverse, 2002): 81. See also D. Spiegel, J. R. Bloom, and I. Yalom, "Group Support for Patients with Metastatic Cancer: A Randomized Prospective Outcome Study," *Archives of General Psychiatry* 38, no. 5 (1981): 527–33.

14   Ben-Shahar, *The Question of Happiness.*

CHAPTER 8

1   S. Kurisu et al., "Tako-Tsubo-Like Left Ventricular Dysfunction with ST-Segment Elevation: A Novel Cardiac Syndrome Mimicking Acute Myocardial Infarction," *American Heart Journal* 143, no. 3 (2002): 448–55.

2   C. Parkes, B. Benjamin, and R. G. Fitzgerald, "Broken Heart: A Statistical Study of Increased Mortality among Widowers," *British Medical Journal* 1, no. 5646 (1969): 740–43.

3   N. K. Valtorta et al., "Loneliness and Social Isolation as Risk Factors for Coronary Heart Disease and Stroke: Systematic Review and Meta-Analysis of Longitudinal Observational Studies," *Heart* 102, no. 13 (2016): 1009–16.

4   J. Holt-Lunstad and T. B. Smith, "Loneliness and Social Isolation as Risk Factors for CVD: Implications for Evidence-Based Patient Care and Scientific Inquiry," *Heart* 102, no. 13 (2016): 987–9.

5   For the research on greater vulnerability to infections, see S. W. Cole et al., "Myeloid Differentiation Architecture of Leukocyte Transcriptome Dynamics in Perceived Social Isolation," *Proceedings of the National Academy of Sciences* 112, no. 49 (2015): 15142–147.

   For the Alzheimer's research, see R. S. Wilson et al., "Loneliness and Risk of Alzheimer Disease," *Archives of General Psychiatry* 64, no. 2 (2007): 234–40.

6   My advice was based in part on the work of Sonja Lyubomirsky, PhD. She conducted a study that followed five women with multiple sclerosis for three years. These women were chosen to be peer supports for other MS patients. The results showed that these peer supporters had diminished depressive symptoms and enhanced feelings of happiness, self-worth, mastery, and personal control. They experienced a "helper's high." See Sonja Lyubomirsky, *The How of Happiness: A Scientific Approach to Getting the Life You Want* (New York: Penguin Books, 2008): 130–31.

7   For a good laugh along these same lines, check out some of the comedy routines from stand-up comedian Jim Gaffigan's show *King Baby*. See *King Baby,* directed by Troy Miller, written by Jim Gaffigan and Jeannie Gaffigan; and performed by Jim Gaffigan (USA: Comedy Central, 2009). Documentary.

8   Research has shown that children from ages 6 to 8 start developing concerns about body image. In one study, more than 50 percent of girls and 33 percent of boys between ages 6 and 8 felt that their ideal weight was less than their current weight. See Seeta Pai and Kelly Schryver, "Children, Teens, Media, and Body Image/Common Sense Media," *Common Sense Media: Ratings, Reviews, and Advice,* January 21, 2015. www.commonsensemedia .org/research/children-teens-media-and-body-image. Accessed June 9, 2017. See also Kelly Wallace, "Kids as Young as 5 Concerned about Body Image," *CNN,* February 13, 2015. www.cnn.com/2015/02/13/living/feat-body -image-kids-younger-ages/index.html. Accessed June 9, 2017.

9   For sake of clarity, the statement posits that attention seeking can lead to self-destructive behavior and not that self-destructive behavior is only sourced in attention seeking. While attention seeking can be the primary motive for many people engaged in self-destructive behavior, there are a plethora of reasons for such behavior outside of attention seeking including, but not limited to, distracting oneself from greater emotional pain, a desire to feel when emotionally numb, self-punishment, etc. Some self-injurers show behaviors in contrast to attention seeking and go to great lengths to conceal their behavior from others.

10   Brené Brown, "The Power of Vulnerability," TED Talk, 2009, https://www.ted.com/talks/brene_brown_on_vulnerability.

11   Ibid.

CHAPTER 9

1   Navy SEALs, "The Past, Present and Future of Unconventional Warfare," accessed May 22, 2017, https://navyseals.com/new/structure/.

2   See B. Akil II, "How the Navy Seals Increased Passing Rates," *Psychology Today,* November 9, 2009, www.psychologytoday.com/blog /communication-central/200911/how-the-navy-seals-increased-passing-rates.

3   See *The Brain,* a History Channel documentary produced by Richard Vagg, 2008.

4   Mental imagery was a key piece of the Navy SEAL Mental Toughness Program. The other components included goal setting, self-talk, and breathing. See also *The Brain,* a History Channel documentary.

5   Akil, "How the Navy Seals Increased Passing Rates."

6   Robert Scaglione and William Cummins, *Building Warrior Spirit: With Gan, Soku, Tanden, Riki* (New York: Person-to-Person Publishing, 1990).

7   Ibid.

8   For more on mental imagery and its impact on sports performance, see Erroll R. Korn, *Mental Imagery in Enhancing Performance: Theory and Practical Exercises* (Amityville, NY: Baywood Publishing Co., 1994): 201–30; and Steven Ungerleider, *Mental Training for Peak Performance: Top Athletes Reveal the Mind Exercises They Use to Excel* (Emmaus, PA: Rodale, 2005).

9   V. K. Ranganathan et al., "From Mental Power to Muscle Power—Gaining Strength by Using the Mind," *Neuropsychologia* 42, no. 7 (2004): 944–56; see also G. Yue and K. J. Cole, "Strength Increases from the Motor Program: Comparison of Training with Maximal Voluntary and Imagined Muscle Contractions," *Journal of Neurophysiology* 67, no. 5 (May 1992): 1114–23.

10   V. K. Ranganathan et al., "From Mental Power to Muscle Power." This research is especially relevant for those suffering from an injury. Research shows that mental imagery practice used three or four times a week can result in improvement in a wide range of activities, and can be a replacement to actual exercise and aid in rehabilitation. See J. A. Stevens and M. E. Stoykov, "Using Motor Imagery in the Rehabilitation of Hemiparesis," *Archives of Physical Medicine and Rehabilitation* 84, no. 7 (2003): 1090–92.

11   While mental imagery can grow muscles, it differs with regard to physical training in terms of the amount of muscle fibers and the size of each fiber. Mental training engages a greater number of muscle fibers since there is more activity in the cerebral cortex. Physical training damages the fibers, causing them to grow back stronger and bigger. For more, see Stephen M. Kosslyn, William L. Thompson, and Giorgio Ganis, *The Case for Mental Imagery* (New York: Oxford University Press, 2006).

12   Yue and Cole, "Strength Increases from the Motor Program."

13   "Natan Sharansky: How Chess Kept One Man Sane," *BBC News*, January 3, 2014, www.bbc.com/news/magazine-25560162.

14   Malcolm Gladwell, "The Physical Genius," *New Yorker*, August 2, 1999, 57–65.

15   For a fuller explanation of the benefits of a process- versus outcome-based visualization, see L. B. Pham and S. E. Taylor, "From Thought to Action: Effects of Process-Versus Outcome-Based Mental Simulations on Performance," *Personality and Social Psychology Bulletin* 25, no. 2 (1999): 250–60.

16   Research has shown that visualization can reduce performance anxiety with regard to public speaking. See J. Ayres and T. Hopf, "Visualization: Reducing Speech Anxiety and Enhancing Performance," *Communication*

Reports 5, no. 1 (1992): 1–10. Visualization has also been shown to reduce anxiety with regard to test taking. See E. Shobe, A. Brewin, and S. Carmack, "A Simple Visualization Exercise for Reducing Test Anxiety and Improving Performance on Difficult Math Tests," *Journal of Worry and Affective Experience* 1, no. 1 (2005): 34–52.

17 Jerry Seinfield, *I'm Telling You for the Last Time*, 1998 performance.

CHAPTER 10

1 Quotes of Michelangelo, accessed February 15, 2017, www.michelangelo.org/michelangelo-quotes.jsp.

2 The self-discovery necessary to develop an identity independent of our circumstances could be an antidote to Impostor Syndrome. Imposter Syndrome is a fear people have that they will be exposed as a fraud in the very area in which they achieved their success. They feel unworthy of their accomplishments and attribute them to being given unfair advantages or being over-evaluated by others. They are afraid they will be "found out." Researchers say this is prevalent in those who come from societies or families that place a heavy emphasis on achievement, as people in these environments yearn for approval but do not feel worthy of it. For more, see P. R. Clance and S. A. Imes, "The Imposter Phenomenon in High Achieving Women: Dynamics and Therapeutic Intervention," *Psychotherapy: Theory, Research and Practice* 15, no. 3 (1978): 241–47. As one starts to discover a self, independent of his or her achievements, there is a profound sense of inner worth that he or she can perceive regardless of the external environment.

3 I first saw this concept mentioned in *The Success Principles: How to Get from Where You Are to Where You Want to Be*, by Jack Canfield and Janet Switzer (New York: William Morrow, 2015), 93.

4 Zig Ziglar, *Over the Top: Moving from Survival to Stability, from Stability to Success, from Success to Significance* (Edinburgh, Scotland: Thomas Nelson, 1997): 1.

5 L. M. Hsu, C. Jaewoo, and E. J. Langer, "The Influence of Age-Related Cues on Health and Longevity," *Perspectives on Psychological Science* 5, no. 6 (2010): 632–48.

6 Ellen Langer, "Do We Need to Stay Sick until Congress Saves Us?" *The Blog* (blog), *Huffington Post*, October 26, 2009, www.huffingtonpost.com /ellen-langer/do-we-need-to-stay-sick-u_b_258631.html.

7 Daniel Goleman, Richard Boyatzis, and Annie McKee, *Primal Leadership: Unleashing the Power of Emotional Intelligence* (Boston: Harvard Business Press, 2013): 115–16.

8   Nehemia Polen, *The Holy Fire: The Teachings of Rabbi Kalonymus Kalman Shapira, the Rebbe of the Warsaw Ghetto* (Northvale, NJ: J. Aronson, 1994).

9   Kalonymus Kalman Shapira, *To Heal the Soul: The Spiritual Journal of a Chasidic Rebbe* (Northvale, NJ: J. Aronson, 1995).

10   There is great research done by psychologist Hal Hershfield, PhD, showing how the practice of envisioning our future selves enhances our decision-making abilities. People who can step into the shoes of their future selves have an increased tendency to make decisions that delay gratification for later rewards, and are more likely to behave in ethically responsible ways, as compared to people who lack continuity with their future selves. See H. E. Hershfield et al., "Increasing Saving Behavior through Age-Progressed Renderings of the Future Self," *Journal of Marketing Research* 48 (2011): S23–S37; and H. E. Hershfield, T. R. Cohen, and L. Thompson, "Short Horizons and Tempting Situations: Lack of Continuity to Our Future Selves Leads to Unethical Decision Making and Behavior," *Organizational Behavior and Human Decision Processes* 117, no. 2 (2012): 298–310.

11   P. A. Mueller and D. M. Oppenheimer, "The Pen Is Mightier Than the Keyboard," *Psychological Science* 25, no. 6 (2014): 1159–68. See also Henriette Anne Klauser, *Write It Down, Make It Happen: Knowing What You Want—and Getting It* (New York: Scribner, 2000).

CHAPTER 11

1   Tom Anderson, "5 Ways to Keep Your Financial New Year's Resolutions," *Forbes*, January 8, 2016; see also J. C. Norcross, M. S. Mrykalo, and M. D. Blagys, "Auld Lang Syne: Success Predictors, Change Processes, and Self-Reported Outcomes of New Year's Resolvers and Nonresolvers," *Journal of Clinical Psychology* 58, no. 4 (2002): 397–405.

2   Norcross, Mrykalo, and Blagys, "Auld Lang Syne."

3   See R. F. Baumeister, "Ego Depletion and Self-Control Failure: An Energy Model of the Self's Executive Function," *Self and Identity* 1, no. 2 (2002): 129–36; K. D. Vohs and T. F. Heatherton, "Self-Regulatory Failure: A Resource-Depletion Approach," *Psychological Science* 11, no. 3 (2000): 249–54; and W. Hofmann, F. Strack, and R. Deutsch, "Free to Buy? Explaining Self-Control and Impulse in Consumer Behavior," *Journal of Consumer Psychology* 18, no. 1 (2008): 22–26.

4   R. F. Baumeister et al., "Ego Depletion: Is the Active Self a Limited Resource?" *Journal of Personality and Social Psychology* 74, no. 5 (1998):

1252–65. See also Roy F. Baumeister and John Tierney, *Willpower: Rediscovering the Greatest Human Strength* (New York: Penguin, 2011).

5   Laura Vanderkam, "Can You Learn Willpower?" *CBS Moneywatch*, September 22, 2011, www.cbsnews.com/news/can-you-learn-willpower/.

6   Dr. Benjamin Gardner, a psychologist focusing on habit research at King's College London, differentiated between habits and habitual behaviors. Gardner stresses the importance of establishing routines, a series of behaviors regularly practiced, to build strong habits. See B. Gardner, "A Review and Analysis of the Use of 'Habit' in Understanding, Predicting and Influencing Health-Related Behavior," *Health Psychology Review* 9, no. 3 (2015): 277–95; see also T. Kurz et al., "Habitual Behaviors or Patterns of Practice? Explaining and Changing Repetitive Climate-Relevant Actions," *WIREs: Climate Change* 6, no. 1 (2015): 113–28.

7   There is a similar reference in Charles Duhigg's book *The Power of Habit: Why We Do What We Do and How to Change* (London: Random House, 2013), which is an excellent resource for understanding the impact of routines on behavior.

8   Daniel Kahneman, *Thinking, Fast and Slow* (New York: Farrar, Straus and Giroux, 2011).

9   James wrote this in his diary in 1870; see Gerald E. Myers, *William James: His Life and Thought* (New Haven, CT: Yale University Press, 2001. James also said, "The great thing, then, in all education is to make our nervous system our ally instead of our enemy." See William James, *The Principles of Psychology* (New York, Henry Holt and Company, 1890).

For a more philosophical exploration of how habit, or "custom," rules our lives, please see David Hume, *A Treatise of Human Nature* (Mineola, NY: Dover Publications, 2003).

10   Stephen King once said, "I like to get ten pages a day, which amounts to 2,000 words. That's 180,000 words over a three-month span, a goodish length for a book— something in which the reader can get happily lost, if the tale is done well and stays fresh." See Stephen King, *On Writing: A Memoir of the Craft* (New York: Scribner, 2000).

11   Leo Tolstoy, *Tolstoy's Diaries,* trans. R. F. Christian, vol. I., 1847–1894 (London: Athlone Press, 1985): 183.

12   Benjamin Franklin, *Benjamin Franklin, His Life* (Boston: Ginn and Company, 1906). For a more comprehensive list of the daily habits and rituals of successful individuals, see Mason Currey, *Daily Rituals: How Artists Work* (New York: Alfred A. Knopf, 2013).

13 Michael Merzenich has conducted extensive research showing the impact of actions on our brains. As we engage in a task, the brain's representation of the specific body parts involved change to adapt to the performance of the task. These changes can affect hundreds of millions of synaptic connections, rewiring cortical maps to the new activity. See W. Jenkins et al., "Functional Reorganization of Primary Somatosensory Cortex in Adult Owl Monkeys after Behaviorally Controlled Tactile Stimulation," *Journal of Neurophysiology* 63, no. 1 (1990): 82–104.

14 Daniel Goleman, Richard Boyatzis, and Annie McKee, *Primal Leadership: Unleashing the Power of Emotional Intelligence* (Boston: Harvard Business Review Press, 2013): 116.

15 Kahneman's research discusses the "law of least effort." People gravitate to the least demanding course of action, both physically and cognitively. Therefore, to make habits stick, one should make them as small as possible. See Kahneman, *Thinking, Fast and Slow.*

16 Based on a conversation between Jerry Seinfeld and Brad Isaac. See James Clear, "How the 'Seinfeld Strategy' Can Help You Stop Procrastinating," *Entrepreneur,* January 27, 2014, https://www .entrepreneur.com/article/231023.

CHAPTER 12

1 Mihaly Csikszentmihalyi, *Flow: The Psychology of Optimal Experience* (New York: Harper & Row, 1990). See also Mihaly Csikszentmihalyi, "Flow, the Secret to Happiness," TED Talk, 2004, https://www.ted.com/talks/mihaly_csikszentmihalyi_on_flow.

2 Csikszentmihalyi, *Flow*; see also S. Prescott, M. Csikszentmihalyi, and R. Graef, "Environmental Effects on Cognitive and Affective States: The Experiential Time Sampling Approach," *Social Behavior and Personality* 9, no. 1 (1981): 23–32.

3 C. P. Janssen et al., "Integrating Knowledge of Multitasking and Interruptions across Different Perspectives and Research Methods," *International Journal of Human-Computer Studies* 79 (July 2015): 1–5. See also P. Bregman, "How (and Why) to Stop Multitasking," *Harvard Business Review*, May 20, 2010; C. Rosen, "The Myth of Multitasking," *The New Atlantis* 20 (Spring 2008): 105–110; and L. Burak, "Multitasking in the University Classroom," *International Journal for the Scholarship of Teaching and Learning* 6, no. 2 (2012): 1–12.

4 C. P. Janssen et al., "Integrating Knowledge of Multitasking and Interruptions."

5   K. K. Loh and R. Kanai, "Higher Media Multi-Tasking Activity Is Associated with Smaller Gray-Matter Density in the Anterior Cingulate Cortex," *PLoS One 9*, no. 9 (2014): e106698.

6   Publilius Syrus was originally a slave, but his wisdom won over his master, who freed him. Some believe that the actual quote was *Duos qui sequitur lepores neutrum capit* (Who chases two rabbits catches neither). See David Macdonnel, *Dictionary of Quotations, in Most Frequent Use* (Whittaker, 1926): 467.

7   Jennifer Senior, *All Joy and No Fun: The Paradox of Modern Parenthood* (New York: HarperCollins, 2014).

CHAPTER 13

1   Bronnie Ware, *The Top Five Regrets of the Dying: A Life Transformed by the Dearly Departing* (Carlsbad, CA: Hay House, 2012).

2   Dan Gilbert, "The Surprising Science of Happiness," TED Talk, 2004, https://www.ted.com/talks/dan_gilbert_asks_why_are_we_happy. Professor Gilbert was referencing a study on lottery winners and paraplegics. Researchers studied the happiness levels of people who have won the lottery and, in contrast, those who suffered a severe accident a year after the event. They found that lottery winners were not happier than the control group, and both lottery winner and controls were slightly happier than paraplegics. See P. Brickman, D. Coates, and R. Janoff-Bulman, "Lottery Winners and Accident Victims: Is Happiness Relative?" *Journal of Personality and Social Psychology 36*, no. 8 (1978): 917–27.

3   David G. Myers and Ed Diener, "Who Is Happy?" *Psychological Science 6*, no. 1 (1995): 10–19.

4   See Anders Ericsson and Robert Pool, *Peak: Secrets from the New Science of Expertise* (Boston: Houghton Mifflin Harcourt, 2016). Dr. Anders Ericsson's research on expertise is centered on constantly practicing outside of one's comfort zone.

5   John Wooden, "The Difference between Winning and Succeeding," TED Talk, 2001, https://www.ted.com/talks/john_wooden_on_the_ difference_between_winning_and_success.

6   Carol Beers, "Book Explores Why People with the Right Stuff Go Wrong," *Seattle Times*, May 14, 1987.

7   Malcolm Gladwell, "The 10,000 Hour Rule," in *Outliers: The Story of Success* (New York: Little, Brown and Company, 2008): 35–68.

8 K. A. Ericsson, R. T. Krampe, and C. Tesch-Roemer, "The Role of Deliberate Practice in the Acquisition of Expert Performance," *Psychological Review* 100, no. 3 (1993): 363–406. See also K. A. Ericsson, "Attaining Excellence through Deliberate Practice: Insights from the Study of Expert Performance," *Teaching and Learning: The Essential Readings,* ed. C. Desforges and R. Fox (Oxford: Blackwell Publishers Ltd., 2002): 4–37; and K. A. Ericsson, "Deliberate Practice and the Modifiability of Body and Mind: Toward a Science of the Structure and Acquisition of Expert and Elite Performance," *International Journal of Sport Psychology* 38, no. 1 (2007): 4–34.

9 It should be noted that a key component of deliberate practice is learning. To develop an expertise, you need to not only know what you did wrong, but how to fix it. In some cases, that can be self-taught, but in order to reach a high skill level, you will need direction from outside instructors.

10 Sean Patrick, *Alexander the Great: The Macedonian Who Conquered the World* (Oculus Publishers, 2013).

11 Melinda Beck, "If at First You Don't Succeed, You're in Excellent Company," *Wall Street Journal*, April 29, 2008.

12 Hamlet 2.2.212

13 S. G. Hofmann et al., "The Efficacy of Cognitive Behavioral Therapy: A Review of Meta-Analyses," *Cognitive Therapy and Research* 36, no. 5 (2012): 427–40.

14 J. Tomaka et al., "Cognitive and Physiological Antecedents of Threat and Challenge Appraisal," *Journal of Personality and Social Psychology* 73, no. 1 (1997): 63–72.

15 In an interview with the *New Yorker*, Ariely states that advising yourself is fraught with biases since your emotions are more likely to cloud your judgment. When we are external to something, we have an easier time looking at it objectively. He said, "When you're in love, you can't imagine the situation will ever change. So you keep on thinking to yourself, *I will always feel this way.* But when somebody else sees you from the outside, they can say, *This is right*, or *This is wrong*, or *Don't do it*, because they're not infatuated. They can see things from a more objective way." See Melissa Dahl, "Why Is It So Hard to Take Your Own Advice?" *The Cut*, June 26, 2015, http://nymag.com/thecut/2015/06/why-is-it-hard-to-take-your-own-advice.html.

16 Viktor E. Frankl, *Man's Search for Meaning* (New York: Simon and Schuster, 1984).

INDEX